MICROGREENS

A Beginner's Guide to Start Your Own Sustainable Microgreen Farm

(The Insiders Secrets to Growing Gourmet Greens & Building a Wildly Successful Microgreen Business)

Melvin Skinner

Published By Melvin Skinner

Melvin Skinner

Microgreens: A Beginner's Guide to Start Your Own Sustainable Microgreen Farm (The Insiders Secrets to Growing Gourmet Greens & Building a Wildly Successful Microgreen Business)

ISBN 978-1-77485-406-8

Legal & Disclaimer

The information contained in this book is not designed to replace or take the place of any form of medicine or professional medical advice. The information in this book has been provided for educational and entertainment purposes only.

The information contained in this book has been compiled from sources deemed reliable, and it is accurate to the best of the Author's knowledge; however, the Author cannot guarantee its accuracy and validity and cannot be held liable for any errors or omissions. Changes are periodically made to this book. You must consult your doctor or get professional medical advice before using any of the suggested remedies, techniques, or information in this book.

Upon using the information contained in this book, you agree to hold harmless the Author from and against any damages, costs, and expenses, including any legal fees potentially

TABLE OF CONTENTS

Introduction

If you're reading this and you are interested, let me say something very quickly You are making a fantastic decision.

It's not just that you're getting into the world of health and well-being, but you're also leading the way in creating something that you can do for yourself. In a time when the world is changing rapidly and quickly, we must decide to adapt to keep up with the times and strive each day to be better than the day before.

This guide has been created for you, those who are striving to new territories and discovering new skills that add value to their lives as well as nurture their minds.

We're here as your companions, encouraging you to do amazing things. We hope that when the book is done and your seeds have developed, you'll be able to utilize this knowledge to assist those around you enjoy the same positive energy and rewards you gained through us.

So Let's get into the subject you sought out when you opened the microgreens book.

Microgreens are the newest seedlings of beans, vegetables seeds, herbs and grains. They have four to six times the nutrients and vitamins than mature leaves of these plants. This comprehensive guide will walk you on how to cultivate microgreens at home cost-effectively and efficiently, making use of the tools you have at home to make your own miniature garden.

A few of us have only a tiny window in our kitchens, or a beautiful patio to plant our seeds. I can assure you that there is plenty of space to grow your own microgreen garden. This is an enjoyable and simple hobby for anyone looking to improve their well-being (both physically as well as mentally) and enjoy the wonders nature can provide.

This book contains complete information and guidance on how on how to choose the right seeds to plant and the correct type of soil. The book also includes guidelines on the right temperatures, light levels and ventilation of your microgreens. We'll also cover strategies to prolong your harvest, methods to prevent contamination from mold or bacteria as well as the best way to preserve your plants and how you can use to supplement your food!

It is packed with helpful tips and vibrant images, this book explores each aspect of this distinctive type of gardening that anyone can get started at inside their homes. This guide is ideal for anyone who is just starting out and wants to dive into the microgreens, and to grow the garden of your dreams.

Alongside everything that was mentioned earlier the book also provides the answer to an crucial question that is at high in our head What is the best way to start a business made of microgreens? If yes, how do I make it happen?

Yes, it's right, you can turn profits from this new hobby! Everything you need to know to get started is on these pages. Everything from where to begin and grow your business, to the most profitable seeds, and finding your first customer.

Don't pass up the chance to enhance your financial situation and lifestyle within a few weeks. You've taken the first step to an improved life. All you need to do is get through to reach the end!

Chapter 1: Microgreens

Microgreens for commercial growers:

Growing microgreens is a strategy to extend the reach of your business to include this into a large unknown market. We've never presented our greens to an expert in the kitchen who was not enthusiastic about making use of the benefits. The enthusiasm is shifting to the showcase for customers and making the request more rooted. Since a growing number of people are experiencing the distinct contrast between crisp neighborhood vegetables, the microgreens are sure to be a huge success. The ability to offer your locals this year-round asset could be a fantastic way to increase your activities. Another benefit these greens provide is the ability to earn fast ranch wages while making it more ripe.

On many farms, it typically takes between a few and a few months before they begin to recover the funds put in fertilized land and manure. Although the ranch's main focus isn't always focused on earning a profit, but instead the health that the property and the encompassing network of roads, steady earnings are crucial to meet the demands of the ranch and homestead family.

Microgreens are a low-cost starting plant and most varieties cost less than two dollars per container of seed and soil. After planting, they'll start producing pay in just some time.

Once your plate is collected, fertilizing the dirt that is now loaded with root and stem matter is similarly quick and easy. When the weather is warm, middle of the year, this dirt is able to be revised as well as treated and then used within a matter of one month. We've designed a unique worm-catcher for this purpose. When our plates are treated with the soil, lots of worm castings are added into the soil, helping it grow even further. It could be used to start your seedlings, and then be consolidated to those fields. It could be being used to create additional microgreens. In all their advantages it is possible to see any reason why microgreens could improve your small ranch.

For Home Growers:

Alongside their incredible flavor and classy appeal microgreens are also extremely nutritious. They can be accumulated and consume them within moments allows you to access their most nourishing and nourishing state. They provide us with a powerful variety of delicious supplements, minerals and phytonutrients. As your taste buds gain to the maximum extent possible from their amazing flavor and a healthy body will reap the advantages of their powerful improvements.

It's quite amazing to eat food so amazing that you feel goosebumps because of how wonderful and fresh it tastes. We've been cultivating food and eating plates with microgreens of mixed greens for a considerable period of time, and the notion of making one for ourselves puts smiles on our faces. We're constantly amazed by how much we can consume all at once. It's similar to drinking a glass of infection water on a scorching day in summer. Your body is at simultaneity with your brain that is, at the moment, is the most beneficial thing you can do.

Microgreens and children:

Growing microgreens isn't just for adults! It can be an fun and enjoyable way for children to connect with the environment. Microgreens help connect children to nature. the outdoors at home or in school, teaching on where the food we eat comes from and the best way to grow it. Children have more of the ability to connect with their surroundings in the event that they're part of the process. Seeds are the seeds that transform in their greens. The persona and the association are formed by the plant and its development. Molly Kaizen portrayed this marvel when she talked about organizing a group of students from school for a visit to "The Pizza Farm" located in northern California. Children spent hours studying and observing all of the elements that made up pizza. The cows that produced the milk that created the cheddar and the fields that grew the wheat which was ground to create the outer layer as well as the growing herb and tomatoes that comprised the sauce. Then they had to make the pizza themselves. The expectation was portrayed by the chef when they believed that their pizza would wrap up. Each one checked every couple of minutes to make sure that their masterpieces were done. This kind of fervor isn't evident when our children's faith in food that is solidified will appear in their food items. It's a blessing when we provide our children with a sense of their food and how it is made. Particularly in urban and rural regions, many youngsters aren't sure where food originates. If one hasn't seen the harvest of a carrot from the ground, what do you know where it came from? It's equally clever to think that a carrot comes from a container or purchased from a store. Starting microgreens with your children lets them get their hands on the soil. They have the opportunity to see the other plants that are growing in the soil. It becomes lively in their brains watching worms eat the kitchen scraps and seeds sprout. It is possible to spot your discerning eaters asking for more greens for their dinner plates! As this living system is thought of and analyzed, the possible outcomes are awe-inspiring. From just a few simple seeds, you can see right out of the box, new eyes to the natural world.

Microgreens are different from. Sprouts vs. Baby Greens:

Microgreens, Sprouts, and greens for children are the entire stages of the development of a plant. Each has distinct characteristics and different the nutritional benefits. Growing is the main stage of a seed's development. "Sprout" is actually synonymous with germinating. It is developed in a variety of chambers, the seeds are kept moist and kept at the temperature of room until they begin to sprout. Instead of allowing them develop in a media and develop to grow into a plant are sucked out immediately once they have sprouted. Usually, they are obscure and produce an icy surface, they've become increasingly famous for their health advantages.

When a seed is the seed is growing in an environment (soil or another thing) The second stage of the seed's development is the laying of its foundations as well as the

12

beginning of its first leaves, also known as cotyledons. The greens that are reaped in this stage are known as microgreens. If microgreens can continue expanding, they place on their next set of leaves, referred to as "genuine leaves." True leaves are the ones of a plant which distinguish it as a different plant. While many brassicas (cabbage broccoli, cabbage, arugula and many more.) all share the same characteristics as heart-shaped cotyledons. However, when their leaves actually form their own distinct appearance, they are and can easily be distinguished by their distinct appearance. The greens are harvested in their beginning stages, and only allowed to grow in dirt until 14 days. They possess all the benefits of sprouts for health and also have the added benefit of the ability to follow minerals that have been accumulated in the soil they're growing in. In this stage, their surface, appearance and taste are more like a dish of mixed greens and greens rather as opposed to a crisp plant. If seeds were allowed to continue growing beyond the stage of the real leaf and in the event of enough evidence it would eventually end up at the stage of infant green. The delicate greens of the child stage which are commonly used in salad plates of mixed greens blends, often referred to as mesclun or spring blend. They are much more delicious and delicate than leaves of the full-grown head of lettuce but do not have the flavor power and health benefits they provided at the microgreens' arranging.

Healthy and microgreens:

As individuals, our primary institutions are in the earth. Yet, we have largely ignored this significant connection in the past almost a century, our relationship with nature has become so outdated and essential that it cannot be disregarded. If, while we're eating, we have an instant break and can at an effort take our food back to the animals, plants and the soil. And even the wind, the deluge and sun. All of these elements have their own place with the land. It is not difficult to see that the sufficiency of the earth as well as the well-being of individuals are tied by and large.

The standard agriculture is used for many years across the globe. Small extension and operated with a hand These farms are increased in size and are well managed. Farmers who are well-trained make the art that is soil management their primary job, and are developing in a manner that helps and enhances the quality of life for the estate, and all and anyone who is in contact with it. The animals that are raised here are shrewd and have thick coats. The earth is fertile, soft and sweet-smelling. The plants are abundant and vigorously grow with no evidence of pressure. The nutrients that are provided here aid in the evening out and wealth to the system that it is incorporated into. It is true that anyone who is a casual observer can detect the "baffling thing" that engulfs the air within an agricultural property.

The bigger a home is in size and the more advanced its mechanical goals the further it drifts from this isolated little farm model. Through the entire last century, there has been an ever-changing shift in the dimensions and the points of convergence in the farming model at the present time. Prior to the conclusion of World War II, it was often believed that cutting technology, mechanized, mechanical structures would be better than the less extensions of traditional methods. The industrial revolution was the first substance fertilizers in the cultivation of crops. Following the war, an enormous portion of the heightens which were used to make bombs of bombs were transformed into manure for plant use.

At this point, the conviction that farms must be huge to make use of the office model of the present took hold. Many farmers moved off their land and joined urban networks to be part of the ever-growing industry. The family farm slowly disappeared because of the massive agri-business that took over.

Through the entire outstanding century that followed, it is estimated that the United States has lost over 4.5 million farms. According to the U.S. specification office, the number of people who live and working on farms has decreased from 40% to less than one percent. Alongside this overhaul of the nation's farms was the inevitable exchange of the notion of having produce readily accessible. In the book by Paul Bergner the Healing Power of Minerals, special Nutrients and Trace Elements, USDA estimations are combined which indicate a decrease. These numbers show mineral and supplement substances declining in a variety of dirt-related results between 1962 between 1962 and 1992. In addition, calcium decreased by around

30%, iron by 32 percent and magnesium dropped at 21 per cent. Produce sustenance is driven by the concept of the soil in which it was grown as well as the manner in which it was obtained and treated after it was collected and also how old it will be when it shows in your fork. To understand the health benefits of microgreens it is important to first examine how these components affect the healthful substance in our food.

Soil and Health:

The interplay between soil and plants are vast and complicated that only a few have dedicated their lives to studying the relationship between them. Based on these researches, researchers confirm what the traditional rancher has believed for many years: variety is one of the key factors to a healthy soil, and consequently robust animals and plants. Yield turns, manures soil corrections, supporting creature cultivating, as well as the emergence of a variety of crops all add to the wide-ranging decent range and ripeness of the soil. The crops that are grown in fertile soil will be awash with minerals, phytonutrients and the follow-up components. Attention to the quality of soil science triggers natural vermin and obstruction to dry season and creates a ranch that is able to sustain life without conclusive proof.

In the horticulture industry soil has been reduced to an element that keeps our plants in place instead of the vibrant powerful force it should be. In the present, soil that is seen as unproductive and second-rate. The Centre is used to promote huge area single-crop development (mono-culture) and wide-ranging compound treatment. In this context the huge amount of soil-enhancing systems is omitted and replaced by the persistent use of three composts that dissolve in water that include nitrogen, phosphorus as well as potassium (N-P-K). The natural life of dirt is severely reduced, compromising its health and the respectability of.

Once this problem has developed beneath the surface, signs start to show up in body of the plant. The nature of the plant's defense against insects, parasites, and other ailments has been compromised leaving it vulnerable and defenseless to assault. The problem is addressed in normal agribusiness through using a broad range of fungicides and pesticides. The results are effective. There are fewer bugs, less disease more generally speaking, less damage for the plants. If you look at it from a distance all the dirt appears dark-colored and the plant in spite of everything appears green. It seems to be an effective, practical method to control these unwanted elements.

Tragically, while the dirt is ignored vegetables are offered heavier and more extensive uses of these toxic substances.

The final blends have to be hazardous in the sense that only unique costumes and veils must be employed to apply these substances. If you were to look at the surface, you will observe the depletion of organic life and possibility of passing the dirt. Once the entire microbiology has gone there is no way that nitrogen or phosphorus or potassium will be able to help bring it back. The soil that was once abundant and productive is no longer suitable to be used for agriculture. The dirt has been transformed into something to treat , as instead of something to build and strengthen. This can be seen in the way medical technology is advancing its understanding of how the body functions. The majority of time is devoted to the patient's symptoms rather than looking at the cause. As infections become more solid, so do bugs. We are constantly expanding our measurements and discover that the root of the problem is present, and the symptoms are becoming increasingly difficult to deal with. A few have found an holistic approach - looking at the entire body, the whole farm, the whole earth to be the answer to both the wellbeing of people as well as the agribusiness. It's becoming more common knowledge that healthy nutrition and a well-functioning lifestyle improve the lifespan and overall health of individuals.

Harvesting and Health:

The efforts of soil and plants are complicated and vast that some people have devoted their entire lives to pondering these issues. Through these studies scientists are reinforcing what the typical farmer has been able to know for many years: grouped selection is one of the most important factors in ensuring a sound soil and , in turn, robust animals and plants. Turns in yield, composts, soil treatments, supporting livestock development, and growth of a variety of vegetables all contribute to the growing variety and readiness of the soil. Produce grown in fertile soil will be awash with minerals, phytonutrients, and follow-up segments. The soil's science and quality triggers regular pests and dry season hindrances creating a farm that could be a source of uncertainty for life.

In traditional cultivation soil is now just the medium used to keep our crops up, instead of the vital incredible force it is supposed to be. In the present the soil of the administrators is regarded as unsustainable and not up to par. The focus is placed on massive expansion single-crop cultivation (mono-culture) as well as a broad scope compound treatments. In this system the large portion of soil-improving frameworks is ignored and displaced by the diligent use of three manure-dissolving water sources including nitrogen, phosphorus as well as potassium (N-P-K). The life-span of the soil is severely diminished trading its abundance and morality.

When the problem has started to manifest beneath the surface, symptoms begin to show up in body of the plant. In a flash, the plants' signature protection from bugs, parasites and illness has been compromised making it vulnerable and vulnerable to ambush. This is a problem that is dealt with in agribusiness that is commonplace by using numerous chemicals, including fungicides. The outcomes appear, according to all indications to be efficient. There are fewer bugs, less sickness and less damage to the plant. For an uninitiated eye the earth, despite everything else, appears dull and the plant, regardless of the surroundings appears green. It creates the impression that it is a competent method of managing these unlucky components.

As the earth is largely ignored, the vegetables are being given more and more of harmful chemicals. Finally, the manufactured creations should be hazardous enough that suit and shrouds should be used for their application. In the event should the possibility arise that you in one way or another were to investigate the soil surface, you will observe the demise of the natural life , and possibly the disappearance of soil. When the entire living organisms has died and gone, there is no amount of nitrogen or phosphorus can restore it. The soil that was once abundant and productive is now prohibited from cultivating. The soil is now an object to be treated instead of something that is built and strengthened. This is evident in the way bleeding edge treatments consider how the body functions. Many hours are spent looking for symptoms, rather than studying the reasons behind. As the emergence of contaminations becomes more established, so are the signs of bugs. We are constantly expanding our estimates only to discover that the underlying issue is there regardless of the circumstances and the symptoms are becoming increasingly difficult to address. There are those who have observed an vastly inclusive approach--looking at all of the body, the entire farm, the entire earth to be the answer to both the human well-being and the agribusiness. It's becoming gradually becoming the norm that good food and a balanced lifestyle can improve the longevity and well-being of the people.

Chapter 2: Famous Microgreens

If you've been interested in the development of your food microgreens can be a great location to start. Professional and novice cultivators have amazing desire.

Microgreens can be cultivated all year round They're extremely cost-effective and usually take longer than a week for the seeds to grow to being prepared for consumption.

Even if you reside within an apartment you could put a few microgreen trays on a window that is sunny.

If you find yourself buying some microgreens at the grocery savings every week If you want to grow them, why not do yourself to save to save some money and gain more understanding of where your food is sourced?

Don't rely on what your tastes are when it comes to the food you eat; there's the perfect microgreen. Most any plant or vegetable could be produced as microgreens.

The options are virtually endless in terms of the kinds of microgreens that you can eat. Each of them is excellent sources of polyphenols and nutrients, so it is very difficult to miss.

Here are some of the most renowned and well-known microgreens that you're likely to find in the nearest store to you:

Arugula

leafy vegetable

If you've ever purchased a spring-inspired salad mix at the supermarket you're probably familiar with the arugula. It's also known as rocket.

This lush green vegetable contains more nutrients, vitamins, phytochemicals and minerals than regular lettuce.

Arugula microgreens are a great choice for keeping your bones strong and healthy. This is because it contains approximately the same amounts of calcium to spinach which is a great chew.

In contrast to spinach, it contains less oxalates which could prevent your body from fully absorbing calcium.

Microgreens in Arugula also have a high content in K-nutrition as well, which is a must to improve bone health.

The antioxidants in the body could also aid in reducing acidity in the belly and also protect against ulcers.

Radish

Radish developing

They're among the fastest growing microgreens and are among the most simple to cultivate at home. Radish microgreens are ready for you to consume in about 12 days after you plant your seeds.

Radish microgreens share the same hot flavor that one would expect when biting into a radish that has grown.

Radish microgreens are extremely high in vitamin C, but they include all types of nutrients and all kinds of nutrients. They also provide a significant amount of protein.

A few people also say that radish microgreens can provide you with a feeling of fullness following their taking in.

The most well-known varieties of radish microgreens comprise of triton Japanese daikons, sango and pink Arrow.

Sunflower

Sunflower microgreens may be the most commonly-used variety can be found in your local farmer's market or at the supermarket next to the radish.

They are a sweet and nutty taste and can be packed with nutrients.

They're abundant and high in B Vitamins, Zinc as well as a variety of minerals and vitamins.

Beetroot

Beetroot grows

Beetroot (typically commonly referred to as beets within North America) are normally cultivated for their roots. They are also great for microgreens, too!

Like arugulaand arugula they're high in vitamin K, which can help prevent osteoporosis, and also assist to clot blood.

Beet microgreens have higher levels of iron than spinach and also provide extra nutritional benefits to help you lose weight. beets that are grown full-time!

Kale

The leaves of kale that have been grown to full size are considered to be superfoods.

In fact, they may be the most highly-rated food on the Aggregate Nutrient Density Index (aka ANDI scale) in terms of nutrient density that is in line with calories.

If you're anything like me, then you can't stand the smell or taste of the leaves of kale. You can, however, eat the leaves in microgreen form and yet reap the benefits of its benefits.

Kale microgreens contain a lot of vitamin C, which could help to keep your immune system in top shape.

Broccoli

Brocolli is growing

Broccoli microgreens are the most potent levels of a chemical that is referred to as sulforaphane, in contrast to virtually every other food available.

Other cruciferous vegetables like the cauliflower and cabbage also have it, however broccoli is the most important source.

Sulforaphane offers some truly remarkable benefits for fitness that have been demonstrated, with many new findings being published every year.

It eases chronic inflammation.

It protects against a variety of types such as neurodegenerative cancer as well as cardiovascular diseases as well as diabetes.

It is also possible to stimulate brain neurons and protect the brain from strokes.

This is why broccoli microgreens have become my preferred type. Each time you consume these, you're protecting yourself from a variety of the most common causes for death , such as coronary heart disease and cancer.

Combine broccoli microgreens

How can cook broccoli microgreens to reap the greatest fitness benefits? The heating process of 70° C for 10 minutes boosts the bioavailability sulforaphane has by about three.5x.

But, if you cook dinner in a hot oven or for a long time, it could ruin the substance eating them raw is a better option when you aren't able to precisely measure the temperature you cook the foods at.

Parsley

Parsley developing

The majority of people view parsley as just a condiment, yet it contains a variety of health benefits.

Parsley microgreens are extremely high in lutein and zeaxanthin, which are essential for proper eye health and to maintain eyesight.

It can also help with asthma, as well as being beneficial to your flow.

Don't think about parsley as the piece of green that is left on your table in your dining area after the meal.

Instead, start incorporating it into your diet by way of microgreens!

Chives microgreens

Chive microgreens possess a mildly onion-like taste. This is due to the fact that the chives are closely linked to onions and garlic.

They contain a chemical called allicin that can boost coronary heart health by reducing the amount LDL (also known as "awful" cholesterol that is present in your blood.

There are anti-inflammatory, antibacterial and anti-bacterial effects of chive microgreens as well.

Mint

Mint leaves

Mint leaves are an essential ingredient in a good mojito. However, they're more than just making cocktails!

With its microgreen appearance mint has some significant health benefits.

It can help alleviate the bad breath, boost mental performance, ease nausea, and even increase the symptoms of irritable bowel syndrome.

Dill

Green Dill

Dill microgreens can ease the intensity of menstrual cramps. Additionally, it has an sedative effect that will help you when you're having difficulty sleeping.

In reality, it's been said that Roman soldiers would apply oil of dill to themselves prior to going into fight to ease anxiety and stress.

Fennel

Fennel vegetable

Microgreen forms of fennel contain nine amino acids essential to life that are proteins essential for repairing and create muscles.

Also, adding fennel microgreens to your weight loss regimen could be a fantastic option following a particularly strenuous workout or when you're an athlete.

It could help those who haven't set to repair damaged tissue

Watercress

The benefits of watercress to fitness

Microgreens from watercress are packed with of all kinds of vitamins. Need diet C? Watercress is more nutritious than oranges.

Also, there is greater calcium content than milk more ferrous than spinach. It also has greater folate than bananas.

As microgreens are extremely very low on calories you'll get many more vital nutrients and nutrients without doubt putting on more weight.

More Microgreens with unusual varieties

Cilantro / Coriander

Two distinct phrases that communicate with the same plant. If you enjoy the flavor of fresh-grown cilantro, you'll also enjoy the taste of it in a microgreen form too.

Certain people love the flavor Some people love the taste, while others hate it, and claim it smells like soap. If you're one of those who do not enjoy the flavor it is possible to put it down to genetics.

Microgreens of coriander and cilantro take between 18 and 20 days to develop.

Cilantro helps stabilize the blood sugar levels of your body, contains plenty of nutrients A, and can even help you the removal of heavy metals of your body.

Mustards

There are a variety of distinct varieties of mustard you can choose from. There are plain green varieties or crimson varieties such as Osaka purple or crimson varieties like a giant pink. However, they all have the same smelly taste of mustard you'd expect.

Microgreens of mustard take between 14 and sixteen days to grow, and reach between 1.5 up to two inches on the top.

There's also an Chinese version of microgreens that you could develop, known as mizuna.

Microgreens from mustard contain high levels of antioxidants. They're also rich in fiber and can aid in detoxifying your blood and liver.

Orach

Orach is a veg that has been around for centuries that is similar to amaranth and the quinoa (which you can also cultivate to grow as microgreens!)

As a mature plant, the leaves are very fleshy and may be bitter, however they are delicious as microgreen. It is a salty mineral type of taste, and some hints of fennel.

Orach helps improve digestion, reduces cancer, enhances kidney function and boosts your immune system to function.

Like spinach, orach is composed of high levels of Oxalic acid. Therefore, you should avoid it if you are susceptible for kidney stones.

Celery

As with all microgreens, celery has the distinctive flavor of the plant grown up you're familiar with.

Celery microgreens contain many minerals and nutrients.

Due to their low Glycemic index, celery microgreens aren't able to raise blood sugar levels or decrease sodium levels.

Moderately difficult Microgreens to cultivate

* Leek

* Beans

* Sorrel

* Celery leaves

* Corn sprouts

* Fennel

* Spinach

* Amaranth

* basil

* Beats

* Chard

* Chives

* coriander

* Cress

What Microgreens Should You Eat?

When it comes to the end at the end of the day picking microgreens is a matter of personal preferences.

It is better to consume vegetables that you truly love instead of having to pressure yourself to eat vegetables that you don't like the taste of.

It's difficult to stick with for a long time in the event you don't enjoy the flavor.

If you prefer a more moderate taste, you can explore broccoli, spinach the cabbage, chard or microgreens of carrots.

If you enjoy the extra flavor of a chunk you can try chives, radishes mint, mustard as well as other stronger-flavored microgreens.

If you're creating your own microgreens It's an excellent idea to choose cool or warm-season flowers based on the time of the season it's in, the temperature and how much sunshine you can get from your home, and other factors.

Microgreens can also be used as a way to test unique greens that you will find in supermarkets, such as tatsoi amaranth, or komatsuna.

Nutrient Microgreens' Assessment

USDA researchers are currently posting an assessment of the nutritional content of 25 readily available microgreens, seedlings of leaves and herbs that have earned the reputation of gourmet food and retail stores. Only a few inches high they have intense flavor and vibrant colors, however what is their nutritional materials?

Nobody knew until this new style was introduced.

We've noticed that baby spinach is one example. has higher levels in phytonutrients than leaves of mature spinach however, what about child spinach, just one week old or old?

Microgreens have a clear advantage (leaves down?) with their significantly higher nutritional density over mature leaves. For instance purple cabbage microgreens possess six times more nutrition C concentration over mature, pink cabbage and 69 times more vitamin K.

Microgreens are healthy, but are best consumed in small amounts. Even the best-quality garnishes will not have a huge impact on your overall health. Microgreens are also expensive. $30 per pounds. You can bring them with you!

There's an ever-changing tray of salads that are cut using scissors.

It's like gardening for the impatient-- absolutely grown in only 7 to fourteen days! If that's not enough What about sprouting? Watch my video Antioxidants sprouting up.

The home-grown sprouts are most likely the most nutritious food-for-cost we can find for the money we spend.

Microgreens (seedlings suitable for consumption as greens and other herbs) have been recognized as a new food trend in the past couple of years. Though they are small in size microgreens may provide surprising flavors, vibrant colors and crisp textures. They could be served as a healthy for eating garnish or as a fresh salad ingredient.

But, no data from a scientific study can be found regarding the nutritional content of microgreens. The current review was conducted to measure the levels of carotenoids, ascorbic acids, phylloquinone and tocopherols in microgreens from 25 different commercial sources.

Microgreen cotyledons have higher nutrition density than older leaf foods (USDA National Nutrient Database). The phytonutrient data can provide a scientific basis for assessing the nutritional value of microgreens as well as contribute to the database of food composition. The information can also serve as a source to health organizations' recommendations and customer's picks for healthy vegetables.

Microgreens' nutritional value

What causes all of it to break down when those youthful, smooth things compete with their more mature counterparts?

Urban Cultivator is presently running on an extensive review of the nutritional impact of microgreens at researchers from the University of Alberta, however when you observe that microgreens percolates, here's an introduction to all the nutritional data you've wanted to know about microgreens and. The mature versions.

Nutritional Information of Microgreens

Red cabbage micros

Six times more vitamin C in the microgreen version (147 mg/245% daily cost in comparison to. 57.5 mg)

40 times extra diet E in microgreen version

69x extra diet K in microgreen version

Cilantro microgreens

Carotenoids higher in the form of carotenoids.

Greater awareness of lutein/zeaxanthin as well as the violaxanthin

3x better in beta-carotene awareness in microgreen version

Garnet amaranth

The highest in nutrition K1 when compared with other microgreens and its matured counterparts

Green daikon radish

The highest amount of vitamin E when as compared to other microgreens, and their mature counterparts

Lettuce seedlings

Most potent antioxidant, particularly after the first seven days of germination. It is superior with other microgreens and their mature counterparts

The highest concentrations of phenolic compounds which promote health, when compared with different microgreens as well as their older counterparts

Sunflower sprouts

Made up of between 24% and 30% protein.

If you look at the nutritional value of these microgreens previously mentioned, there is any reason to not include microgreens in your diet plan to lose weight. It's often hard to obtain the vitamins and minerals you need every day, but, as you can see above, eating microgreens can be the ideal way to accomplish it.

Microgreens take shorter time to develop, and are usually capable of harvesting in seven or 10 days. Contrast this with the time that their more advanced counterparts require -- around eight to ten weeks

It is the Nutritional Properties of Microgreens

Microgreens may not be only suitable for a nutritious soup or salad. Studies on microgreens have found that these tiny, fantastic greens for younger people are superfoods stuffed with a variety of essential vitamins for fitness.

The young and healthy humans seedlings possess astonishing nutritional qualities. Here are the food properties of microgreens.

1. Vitamin C in abundance

Young herbs and greens contain a significant amount of diet C. The crucial diet serves as an antioxidant which allows to eliminate unfastened radicals from your body. The most minimal amount of diet C can be found in a seedling's young age is 20 milligrams for every 100 grams.

The tomatoes themselves don't contain these levels of Vitamin C. It is possible to discover 10 milligrams of nutritional C inside mature tomatoes. This is about half the amount microgreens are able to provide! Microgreens like Crimson cabbage can have as high as 147 milligrams of nutrients C that is comparable to 100 grams.

2. Beta-Carotene

Carotenoids are extremely important in reducing the likelihood of developing illnesses, such as eye diseases and cancer. Beta carotene is one the most significant carotenoids. Micro Green contains large amounts of beta-carotene. In this case micro carrots are a source of 12 milligrams beta-carotene equal to 100g.

3. The source of Vitamin E

Alpha-tocopherol as well as gamma-tocopherol which comprise the nutrition E, can be found in huge amounts in microgreens. The top microgreens according to of E levels in nutrition include Daikon radish. They are a good source of vitamin E, which is in line with 100 grams. A tiny amount of this microgreen will provide your body with the daily requirements of this vital vitamin.

4. Vitamin K

Research has shown that when seeds are exposed the sun, they start creating huge quantities of nutrients K. The vital vitamin acts in the role of an electron acceptor in order to aid chlorophyll in taking in sunlight and transport carbohydrates. For people eating this type of diet, it helps in blood to clot. It also aids in maintaining strong dental bones as well as healthy tooth.

Microgreens have the highest concentration of microgreens. They can contain up to 4.1 micrograms that are vitamin K that is consistent with grams. If you want to obtain the right amount of diet K as well as other vital vitamins that are required using the frame, you must include microgreens in your healthy diet.

Chapter 3: The Materials Utilized In The Cultivation Of Microgreens

Microgreens can be grown with just the use of a few items or materials. There may be several of these in your home, while others require an investment.

Trays

Because microgreens only spend a brief period of time in their containers They can be grown using the use of a shallow jar. Small black plastic bowls of 20x10 inches work very well. They are generally sold for about two dollars per tray at shops that sell gardening equipment. If you are a member of an area nursery, you can go there for containers that would otherwise be discarded. We've seen them during spring, when the local nursery gets small packets of annual flowers in containers of the same size and that they're useless.

If we didn't find this particular niche, we would have had decades of trays, which could have been an additional expense. They stack easily, are easy to use and durable. They can be reused by stacking two together until they begin to crack. Wood is another option. Another option. They'd work equally perfectly if the idea to build your containers from wood. It is also possible to use an old baking pan by cutting a few trousers and lay them on the ground and drain. It's a tiny light, compact, and lightweight rack that you're looking for.

A low-lying flower pot can be an alternative option. If you are choosing a container to plant your microgreens there are a few things to take into consideration. Although they are easy to locate clay pots may hinder germinating by drying the moisture quickly and wicking it away off the soil. Choose a deep, large pot over a large one to increase your greens surface area as well as reduce unnecessary use of soil. You may want to consider using multiple pots as the yield might be less than if you use one tray. It is essential to properly drain regardless of whether you decide to utilize plastic, wood or steel. Though often neglected drainage is among the most important factors in the development of your plant. It's more important for your trays, but essential for the gardens. It is likely that you have a hole cut into the bottom of the tray if you purchase or have a collection of plastic tray. When you make your trays, ensure that the excess water flows through the slits and holes. If there isn't enough drainage, the greens may suffer from reduced growth, redness and the possibility of mold.

Soil

The core of every farming or gardening operation is its soil and that includes microgreens too. It is essential to select the correct soil for your microgreens can flourish. Bio-mineral interactions that are required to produce vibrant, nutritious plants require a lively fertile soil. Apart from some elements derived from the surrounding environment and plants, they are also derived from soils and also water to provide all of their nutrients.

We experimented with a variety of potting soils during our first year of growth, using microgreens and trying to find the best of them. We were amazed by the differences in these research studies. The soil we used was identified as "organic" with components such as bat, earthworm guano and compost, and the list goes on. As our plants grew in these soils the rate of germination growth, development along with overall health issues among plants increased rapidly. In the end, when it comes to maintaining the thick growth of greens, the majority of dirtiest soils made of similar ingredients do not meet.

Both the quality and the production of the soil included additional sea ingredients, such as crab meal, kelp and shrimp meal. While you may be able to make use of a less robust soil however, your microgreens usually require more. You can expect an even, solid growth and a higher yield with high-quality soils. Although the yield per tractor is not as important for the backyard grower but this aspect must be considered by a commercial gardener. The price of better quality soil is usually absorbed through the return on your tray. We recommend that you visit the local nursery or garden retailer and examine the different options available for some time. Speak to storekeepers and pick two pots of soil to take home to test. Be sure the bags contain the ingredients listed to ensure you are aware of what you will get.

Soil Press: You'll require a tool to create an even seedbed once the trays have been filled with soil. We began by trying to grow the greens and then cut out in what we wanted our containers to look like a large sheet of cardboard. It worked in the short-term. But this was due to the harsh weather conditions and the wet tray that damaged them and softened over the longer term. The best choice is to use cardboard for those who sew only several tray at a time and you're not sure if it has to be replaced each time. Cardboard can be found easily and is generally reliable. I wanted a longer-lasting press for our company as we expanded. I came across some wood pieces and constructed an industrial press that had a handle, instead of making a new one of identical material.

Seeds

Another aspect of cultivating microgreens is the quality the seeds. Space handling, age and the source of your seeds are all factors that impact the quality of the seeds you plant. The differences between a germination percentage of 95 percent and a germination rate of 50% can be seen in the event that you sow a hundred thousand seeds. It can be depressing to find that only a tiny portion of your seeds grow up after seeding and caring for your tray.

You should keep the seeds dry and fresh when handling and processing them. Avoid high temperatures and humidity variations. Make sure not to put your seeds in the sunlight or let them become stuck in a summer storm on hot and humid summer days. A proper treatment of the seeds is essential to ensure its longevity. Important information like the time of germination, the age of the plant and the variety of seed are included in seeds' packages. If you do not keep your seeds in a particular location your seeds are dependent on the plants that last between two and five years. The life span of the seeds is standard and will depend on whether you keep them in the correct conditions.

A multitude of seed companies are available at your fingertips through Internet access. Are you searching for companies selling seeds that offer bulk sales to grow microgreens. A lot of companies only offer tiny seed packets can be found in your local garden shop. Start with a tiny amount of seeds when you start an enterprise. Numerous companies will provide free samples upon request. It's likely you'll need to convert to quarter-pound bags after you've discovered the kinds you're looking for.

If you observe it is fast the majority of companies offer up to five pounds of discounts. Price is an issue due to the quantity of seeds you need to go through. Commercial farmers are naturally moving through a little more seeds than the typical plant. So, they will have to browse around to find the most cost-effective quality combination.

There are additional companies offering organic and alternatives that are not organic when you browse through catalogs of seeds. We support small local, organic, and local seed suppliers, however, they're not always accessible or affordable. In addition, trustworthy seed companies that focus on service need to find seeds that are not treated. The unique aspect of rising Microgreen is that seeds not only incredibly germinated they also germinate simultaneously. Certain seeds from our collection have been able to demonstrate the phenomenon known as wave sprout.

There are a variety of variations in the time of sprouting , but they are growing with these seeds. We discovered in between our first and the final seeds, the germinated seed lasted for between two and three days. The majority of those who cultivate large quantities of vegetables aren't aware of this fact. Since we can only take our greens in about a week or so after sprouting, all our seeds must be at the same time to "pop."

The effectiveness of seeds also play a part in the process of transferring seeds. We have grown broccoli with great germination, but horrible cotyledons. I experienced China rose radish which is generally beautiful pink-shaped micro-green and white stems. Also, I had purple cod that ranged from deep purple, to smooth green. These variations may not be a problem for the housekeeper, however these inconsistencies could cause confusion for commercial growers.

Towels

Cloth or paper towels is a quick and efficient alternative to allow the seeds being covered in soil. The typical method is to cover a tray with a clay lump that is enough to completely cover seeds. Cloth towels are ideal for home gardeners who is able to use a washer.

Fabrics made of cotton that are thin and light is recommended. It is recommended to wash them regularly since wet towels could cause mold and bacteria. Paper towels have been extremely successful in our commercial services. The quantity of trays we plant each week has been a superior alternative using paper towels. Paper towels are a great fit in between composting and putting them the vermiculture tank.

Make sure to purchase natural, unbleached paper towels since you don't intend to scrub the seeds that are germinating and the soil with bleach or any other chemicals. The aim, no matter what kind of towel you choose to use is to make sure the seeds remain moist and warm prior to their germination.

Watering Equipment: Hoses, Sprayers and watering Cans

There are already products to water your greens in case you have a tiny garden or a plant in your house. If you plant outdoors, it is vital that you have an appropriate garden bed as well as an irrigation system with several options. Be sure that the frequency of spray can be altered. Medium showers are the most effective of settings for our sprayer. You will require a watering pot for if you plan to be growing inside. It should have fittings that allow the water splash around and not flow in one tube. If you are growing the greens in such a huge amount it is essential to ensure that there is air circulation. It isn't a good idea to soak them in water so much that they're falling over and becoming a mat. When this occurs, they'll be rotting due to a lack of oxygen and water. You can try brushing them straight with your fingers or, in other words "fluff" them when you observe that your greens are falling. The smooth and consistent irrigation is vital.

The pH Meter

A pH meter can be a major investment to make microgreens. The measurement of acidity or alkalinity of the solution is called pH. The degree to which your greenness is able to get the nutrients from the soil determines what your pH is. The nutrients are locked up and inaccessible to vegetation when your pH becomes too high or low. The cost is between $8 and $80 meters. The cheapest options rely on the use of liquid solutions and color matching while the more expensive meters are usually automated and are able to be placed into the water being tested. It is difficult to emphasize enough the importance of having a way to determine the pH of the water. I didn't know about the special pH requirements for many of our plants during the first two years of our operation.

I was also unable to discover the contradictory nature of some crops like beet amaranth, basil, and beet. In a few of the trays we tested, we have experienced slow growth and rot. We had to alter various factors in our system to correct these issues. It was not clear if there was anything that could be done to help us in the long run. In the event that we find similar issues in future seeds, will we get different positive outcomes. I spoke with the proprietor about our displeasure when purchasing soil at the local horticultural store. He suggested that our water's pH be monitored and tested.

Our water that was eight meters deep, was extremely alkaline. I learned this. While I could manage the high pho levels in the Asian vegetable, it was when I discovered that the plants I experienced difficulties reading preferred to be significantly less. After I had adjusted to their needs and stopped swelling, redness, and slow growth. It's been as magical.

However, I was awestruck by the change the pH of our greens have made. To alter pH, you need chemistry to play. A wide range of organic ingredients can be used to decrease or raise pH. One simple method is to lower pH making use of a little citrus juice (increase of acidity).

Baking soda and oyster shells or dolomite lime can raise the pH (increase in the amount of alkalinity that your water has). We have said before that the plant will pull the main nutrients from the soil once pH is set in the right levels for the crop. With this new element in my control I am able to cultivate my greens to their natural leaf-level. The greens have reached an entirely new aesthetic level instead of being slowed down and stressed. However, I believe that the pH monitoring is beneficial and could yield impressive outcomes, it could seem like an additional step. The chapter on individual crops outlines the crops that are susceptible to high pH.

Lids to help germinate

It is possible to purchase or construct containers to protect your tray even if you don't have an existing greenhouse in which to grow. This results in the "mini-greenhouse result" and helps maintain the temperature more consistently and humidity than if the germinating seeds were exposed to outdoor conditions. In dry climates and seasons it's particularly crucial in the case of temperature fluctuations between the hours of day and night. If you do not use lids, germination may be drastically reduced, inconsistent and much less than covered tray. It's well worth the cost to get a good return.

If you purchase an hat, any garden shop or school will have it. You can search online for them in the event that they aren't accessible in your area. The average cost is around $3. Make sure you get an lid that fits inside the container. A advantage is that you are able to locate decks that work in a standard size tray. Consider this when you are planning to build your own trays, or even the flower pot. You'll need to create your deck from scratch in the event that you choose to use an item that has a different dimensions or shape. It is possible to make use of plastic bags or glass panels to do this. If you use them, make sure the lids of plastic are shaded to ensure that the plastic won't break and ruin the appearance of the lids. If glass panels are utilized, keep the heat from getting too hot by keeping the racks out from direct sunlight.

Heat Mats

For plants that thrive in warm weather (such like amaranth and basil) heat mats can give extra warmth or help in the process of germination for any seeds. Sometimes , they're not necessary but they could aid in the germination of colder-weather seeds. In local horticultural shops , or on the internet, heat mats that vary in size and cost are quite affordable. They are powered by electricity and heat the soil from below gently.

Scissors for harvesting

Scissors are a great method of harvesting microgreens I would say. It's an excellent idea to get a different pair for the day of harvest as they're sharp, clean and easy to cut. With the various size of cutting tools, it could also be helpful to cut different types of green density. In this case, sharpness is the primary consideration. If the scissors continue to diminish, they can purchase new scissors or sharpen the one that is in use.

I've recently come across one that is extremely effective after years of experimenting with different sharpeners for knife and scissors. The issue with many manual sharpeners is that they cannot keep the slope in a steady angle throughout sharpening. If the slope's angle isn't maintained the ability to maintain a sharp blade becomes more difficult with time. The sharpener clamp I recently found fits at the side of any scissor bladder or knife, permitting you to sharpen your bladder on a continuous basis. It requires little effort to sharpen your weapon. Clean stems are an important aspect of the green's durability. The less cell damageis there, the longer it can last in the harvest. After the washing process is completed the stems of greens are removed to allow for clean cutting. If they are preserved for use later on the flower stalk may have been cut incorrectly, damaged and stained.

Scale

For those who wish to market their vegetables require an appropriate scale. A variety of options are accessible online, as well as art supply stores at your local eateries. The cost ranges from 40 to 400 dollars. It is important to be precise when selecting a scale. It is important to choose the scale that can give you readings of 1/10 ounce increments when you handle ounces as well as the fraction of an ounce.

Fan

Any normal-sized fan that has a couple of settings will work well for drying greens that you're planning on selling or holding. There's a chance that you'll have a pivoting head that is on the ground or it could be able to guide directly to the drying greens. We suggest that the delicate microgreens you have get dry in low or medium climate.

Storage Containers

You can store your harvest greens in a variety of ways. You can utilize resealable food grade containers or plastic clamshells when you are planning selling your vegetables. These are all available in huge quantities from different vendors. A sealable container or bag is suitable for growing greens for use at home. Treat your microgreens like a delicate leaf salad.

Chapter 4: Growing And Preserving Your Microgreens

The Equipment You'll Are Looking For

We now know something about what microgreens can do It is now time to get into our own gardening process. It can be a enjoyable thing to do and ensure that we're prepared to tackle all of the gardening we wish to continue to grow the microgreens that we have in our homes.

There are numerous tools that can prove helpful when trying to increase the size of our microgreens. Some of them will be crucial, and you should purchase these even for the simplest of microgreen garden that you want to concentrate on. However it is possible to work with more advanced alternatives in the occasion of need. These can help you when you decide to make your the garden larger or want to observe some results in how these microgreens behave.

You are able to choose which one of the items from our list works best to help you build a strong garden and ensuring that you have one of the most beautiful gardens that you can for your personal requirements. The tools suggested for you to start your own microgreens plant include:

35 percent food-grade hydrogen peroxide. This can be an ideal option if you'd like to apply a top spray to the seeds during germination, or when you are planning to rinse the seeds prior to germinating.

Planters: Many times gardeners choose to plant their microgreens in. If you decide to do this then select a good selection of planters. Be sure they're appropriate to meet your requirements and allow enough space for the microgreens to develop. They might be smaller than the traditional vegetable However, you can't put them in a squishy way otherwise they will not grow.

Soil: If you grow outside you can check the pH of your soul and ensure whether it contains the correct type of nutrients that you need for your plants. If you are planning to plant inside, or you find the soil you have isn't enough for microgreens then you are able to get a good quality soil to use inside your home to aid your plants to grow.

Lights: If intend to plant your microgreens inside, it's a good idea to purchase some light sources. The sun is wonderful however since it's difficult to find windows in the home that can allow the plant to be satisfied with the proper quantity of sunlight, buying lights and using those can be the most effective alternative. Choose a top-quality product in case you decide to go this route and make use of these for the appropriate time during the day to assist in helping the plants grow.

pH tester that is waterproof It is crucial to ensure that any water you supply to the greens is at the proper pH. Choose a durable one that will last for a long time and resists water.

The heat mat is another device can be used in the process of germination for your greens. In the process of germination, you have to supply the seeds with ample heat, which will make it much easier.

A timer for your lights: If you're growing your plants in a greenhouse and you are not using a greenhouse, then you need to utilize some heating lights to aid in their growth and become stronger. A timer can make it easier to switch the lights off and on according to the correct time for your plants, without having to keep track of every minute. It is best to set 18 hours of on and off in this.

Pressure sprayer: It does not have to be super robust to be effective; it's only necessary to be user-friendly. This can be used to aid in topping spraying your microgreens as they begin to germinate.

Tweezers: This is an additional tool that you might want to utilize to ease the process of plant. The tweezers are a great tool to plant seeds properly.

A water pitcher can be an excellent tool for the bottom of your microgreens to be watered as needed.

• Strainer - Strainer one that you have in your home, so that it's clean, or buy one specially for this. This will allow you to remove some of the seeds you've got.

Gloves: You'll have to wear these gloves at any time you'll need to handle hydrogen peroxide or when working in a thriving environment that is clean to get the most effective outcomes. Make sure you have gloves only intended to garden.

Security glasses: They don't have to wear them constantly Many gardeners decide not to wear them all the time. They can be useful when making use of the food-grade hydrogen peroxide, which we discussed in the first place. They can help you remain protected.

Syringe: This is an excellent option in the event that you require some pH-balancing in your water. It is usually enough to add only a couple of drops at a given time, so this could make the process much more straightforward.

Citric acid , or lemon juice from organic sources: They are excellent alternatives that are natural and can assist in lowering your pH levels of the water you drink without worrying about it causing harm to your plants.

These are only a few of the fundamentals can be utilized to get your microgreens set for use and to ensure that you're likely to be able to grow your plants according to your preferences. There are more sophisticated options that you can select when you go into a retail store or browse online, you're bound to discover at least some of these to select from. It is important to conduct your own research and determine which is worthy of your attention, and which products are able to deliver on their promises and which best fit the goals you wish to achieve. After that, you'll decide whether you want to use the product or not.

Growing microgreens is an enjoyable experience that everyone will enjoy. It is just a matter of making sure we have the appropriate tools and equipment prior to the time we want to make it as efficient as is possible. If you're prepared to begin growing get out and purchase some of the equipment that will be required to complete this procedure, return to this site and figure out how to tackle the other steps!

A Step-by-Step guide to Growing Microgreens

When you have all the necessary equipment from above, it's time to get started and take a look at the steps can be used to develop these microgreens. You will have some success in the process. Growing microgreens is an enjoyable and rewarding task which you can carry out at your home. If you're looking to save money or just want to include more greens to your diet, you'll be able to find an excellent option to try.

There are many ways can be used to cultivate these microgreens. A majority of people select between a hydroponics setup and soil. The one that is effective most effectively is soil, and we will begin by focusing on how you can do this using a soil-based system. Then, in the end, we will look at the different features in a hydroponic system. The basic steps we'll follow to begin the process of growing our microgreens includes:

Pick the microgreens we'd like to make use of.

* Select the appropriate medium and tools

* Plant your seeds on an evenly distributed manner.

* Add plenty of water

* Take them outside to catch the sun's rays.

• Cut the food and then eat it

Picking Out Your Microgreens

Let's begin. We must begin by looking at the most effective methods for picking microgreens. If you're new to this, you might be interested in knowing how to select the best ones and even how they taste. There are over 100 kinds of microgreens to choose from, which could make choosing difficult. The best way to start by choosing by the type of vegetables you typically are fond of. That means some choices such as chickpeas, arugula sunflower, kale, and broccoli could be great alternatives to consider.

These options are easy to make use of and typically provide the nutrients you'd like. Once you've mastered how to cultivate them options, you can look at something somewhat more challenging. For instance, you could discover that flaxseed or Chia are excellent alternatives. The seeds will develop into an emulsion-like membrane when they are wet, making seeds difficult to work with.

There are other microgreens which can be beneficial, however they take a amount of time to sprout. This could include choices such as lovage and oregano. These are microgreens that resemble herbs, for example, the micro-herb. If you're concerned about choosing a product based on how much nutritional value is contained of it. If this is essential to you, you have to select microgreens that contain more nutrients in them.

One thing you might enjoy here is some hot microgreens. Perhaps you don't want to plant all your garden in this manner but incorporating them will allow you to make modifications to your food They can also are delicious too. A few of the microgreens that can be classified as microgreens and are delicious include:

The purple delight plant The purple delight basil an incredibly spicy and sweet flavor It also has plants that have purple leaves and it takes just about a month to grow.

- Red giant mustard This variety will take about one month to develop as well . It also has red veins and is hot as well.

Lemon basil: This is unique because the flavoring is hot lemon. It grows in the month of July and features vibrant leafy greens that appear stunning in salads.

Ruby streaks mustard This is a fast plant to grow and will take two weeks to finish. It's sweet and spicy flavor too.

If spice isn't your style there are alternatives. You can choose something more gentle and earthy. There are several choices in celery and beet and other microgreens that complement this one. Some of the choices that offer the same flavor they include:

Microgreens of celery: These can take up to up to four weeks before they mature, and will come with a mild, pleasant flavor.

Bull's blood beet It is a kind of taste. It takes about up to a month for it to develop.

Dark purple mizuna It will taste a bit like mustard. It can take about two weeks to develop.

- Hong vit the radish variety: This is similar to radish If you enjoy that flavor and takes about two weeks to mature.

If you've made a decision on which varieties you want to plant, it's easy to get the seeds from your local farmer or gourmet supermarket. If you're not close to one of these places, you will usually be able to find them on Amazon and be able to plant these plants successfully.

Making the Right Choices for the Medium and Tools

We have talked briefly earlier about some of the tools, but it's time to discuss these tools in more detail. We'll discuss the best way to accomplish this in the form of a tray that is about 10x20 inches, so the microgreens can be placed on this. They are available in the local supermarket as well as on Amazon. It is best to verify that the tray has holes inside it. If it doesn't, you need to make a few inside. This will assist you in get rid of the extra water, and also keep the seeds from getting flooded.

Soggy and overwatered soils could cause some issues which include the growth of mold. It is important to ensure that you are working with a high-quality soil that has many good nutrients. You can find it at your local garden and home center to ensure that your microgreens get a excellent conditions, with plenty of nutritious nutrients to thrive in. Be sure to purchase enough soil to fill your pots or trays.

Another option is to purchase a small amount of coconut coir and mix it to the mix of potting. This can help retain the water and improve airflow. It's optional but you could grow your plants without it, however it's beneficial when you are working in seed propagation. If you are using coconut coir, complete filling all of your containers with approximately 3/4 of the potting soil and follow up with coconut Coir.

The source of light you intend to use is crucial. If you are in a warmer climate then you'll already have ample sunlight in your house and you could place the container with seeds close to a bright window. If you reside in an area that's more chilly and you intend to plant the microgreens inside it is possible that you will have to add artificial lighting to help the plants develop in the manner you'd like.

If you must choose using artificial lighting then you must ensure that the light is at least 4 inches above the tray with microgreens. It is possible to make use of a shop light that has fluorescent bulbs for this task if you wish to reduce costs. If you have more money to spend alternative, you could also go using all-flash light bulbs that are fluorescent. These are pricier but will allow your plants grow an extra bit as well.

The Seeds are being sown

Now is the time for us to move on to plant the seeds we intend to use. It is possible to take the container you wish to use and place the soil inside. Be sure to fill the container with around 2 inches of soil in the ratio of three quarters of potting soil to one quarter coconut coir we spoke about earlier. It is possible to lightly rub on the soil in order to make the surface as flat as is possible but avoid making it too compact.

It is the next thing to do looking at the specific instructions included in your seed packet. This is helpful as there may be additional directions to follow as you prepare to start propagating the microgreens. This will let you know the depth you need to plant the seeds and also how time it will take for them to grow. If there are specific instructions or tips to follow regarding the microgreens you'd like to experiment with, they will be included on the instruction for you to follow.

It is now time to scatter the seeds onto the top of the soil you have chosen. You should put around a handful of seeds in your palm and place your hand, holding the palm upwards and at an angle of about a quarter, on the soil's surface. Utilize fingers like your index as well as your middle finger, to slowly distribute seeds while they are being released from your hands. One thing you should try to do is spread seeds in the most extensive way possible.

If you're working with seeds that are smaller you must aim for 10 seeds to every inch.

If you're working with seeds that are larger the ratio should be more like five seeds or more per square inch.

Once you have all the seeds planted all set to be planted, add a small layer of vermiculite, or soil. If you have vermiculite, you may utilize it in place of soil. Vermiculite is a rock that helps in the propagation of seeds. Once you've applied the thin layer it is possible to see some seeds since our aim isn't to cover them completely, rather, to cover them for a while.

It is now time to sprinkle on some water. Seeds won't develop properly if you don't feed them well. They are like all other plants and are awestruck by water. A mister is an excellent method to begin here so they can be soaked without drowning them as you begin. It is essential to mist the greens at least once per day. If you're unsure whether they require more water, place your finger in half an inch of soil. If you feel that the soil is dry it is time to water your greens. If the soil is damp, that's an indication that the seedlings are happy. If you notice that the soil appears to be muddy or even wet, you're watering them too excessively.

It is possible to cover the tray you'll use to build the greenhouse of your dreams. If you are using a propagation tray, then you just need to put another tray over the one you have. If you're using another kind of container, look into a plastic bag with holes. This can create an attractive greenhouse effect, and still allows air to enter.

Chapter 5: How To Prepare And Eat Microgreens

In the previous chapter you were taught how to correctly plant and collect microgreens. But, you're doing it all for the sake of eating healthy and enhancing your diet. In order to achieve this, it's essential to be aware of how to take proper good care of the plants once they've been harvested and to incorporate them into your food plan.

Microgreens contain a lot of nutrients, however but they are also extremely susceptible to conditions in the environment which can rapidly deplete them of vital nutrients. To prevent this, this chapter will provide specific instructions on how to not just store, but also consume microgreens in a healthy method.

In the beginning, we'll talk briefly about the storage of microgreens after harvesting in order to preserve its freshness, taste and nutritional value. You're likely to not consume the whole batch of your vegetables once they've grown. This is the reason you should only collect and keep the amount you're planning to use immediately. It is common for people to collect the entire tray then cool the plant material.

But, this isn't the best method of preserving nutrientssince these plants are extremely perishable and rapidly lose nutrients after harvesting. To ensure that you get the most nutrients, it's important to consume them right away or properly store them. In order to harvest microgreens, is essential to use a sharp, precise instrument. It is recommended to employ ceramic cutting tools or a knife made of ceramic. Ceramic is a nontoxic , non-flammable substance which is delicate and soft. It will not alter chemically with nutrients found in the greens.

It's the same about metals. For instance, if you are using an old, scraped knife, it could affect your herb's health and decrease the nutritional value of your herb. In addition, iron may release ions into your plant, which may speed up the process of the process of oxidation.

Following this, the plants could turn become brown and lose their flavor and nutritional properties. It is important to clean the trays you are growing in after harvesting to eliminate any biofilm or other pollutants which may form in the growth phase. Make use of soap and water, and scrub the trays using the help of a cloth, brush or pressurized water. Then , rinse the trays in water and spray them with a 3percent peroxide solution, or a 5-10% vinegar, or wash them in bleach solution. Rinse thoroughly and dry before the next time you use them.

Another thing to think about is to moisten and allow air to circulate around the plants. This means that you should not keep microgreens in bags that are sealed.

They will be completely depleted of air and they'll begin to deteriorate and degrade faster in these conditions. Instead, give them enough moisture and adequate air circulation. When you are preparing your items to store, lay the produce on an old towel or store them in a storage container.

When you store microgreens, it is recommended that they be protected from direct light, which will reduce their nutritional value. If you're not planning to eat the crops in fresh form then you must store them shaded and shielded from direct sunlight. If properly chilled microgreens will maintain their freshness for approximately one week.

However, it is essential to keep the temperature in the refrigerator below 40 degrees Fahrenheit approximately the temperature of four degrees Celsius. It is not recommended to put microgreens in the freezer. Some studies discovered that microgreens stored at around 40 degrees Fahrenheit could last for up to 21 days. A warmer temperature can reduce this duration to as little as 14 days.

However, this is largely dependent on the type of refrigerator, which means that certain models will be more durable than other. Remember that the use and usage of refrigerators and opening them can alter the temperature for a short time. To ensure that your plants are in good shape be sure to observe the way your stored plants appear. If they start to lose their color to brown, turn brown, or begin to smell oddly then throw them away. This could indicate that they've started to decay or become in a moldy state.

But, many people believe that microgreens can be preserved with plastic containers, too. There are many ways to store microgreens, such as the plastic bag, containers are more likely to keep them fresher for longer.

Clamshells seem to yield the most effective results. Microgreens typically remain fresh for a minimum of one week inside the clamshells. However, it's possible that this period could extend to up to two weeks, depending on the temperature, humidity and the specific kind of.

While bags can be helpful for preserving, they also are also prone to becoming moldy, as it is much more easy for water to condense around plants and create the conditions for microbes thrive. However Clamshells can protect your microgreens from getting squashed and give them sufficient air and space.

If you seal the clamshells correctly and seal the containers and sealed, you can greatly increase the longevity and the freshness that your plant will enjoy. On the other hand glass containers have been found to be not to be effective in protecting the delicate babies of the plant.

To do this, it's crucial that the containers be sterilized. But, they can cause condensation to increase, which could impact the health of your micro-plants. Condensation creates a fertile soil for bacteria and mold. Additionally, glass containers can deplete plants of flavor and smell and preserve freshness. It is important to avoid using single-use plastics as well as Tupperware also.

While these containers may maintain freshness for two weeks, it's possible that their quality could begin to decrease.

Another crucial thing to take into consideration is finding the best location in your refrigerator for you're storing. The different areas of the fridge will have the identical temperature. For example, if your place them in the highest shelf, close to your freezer, lower temperature could cause freezing of the plants.

It is crucial to keep them out of the cooling vent. It is where temperatures most frequently fluctuate. It is best to store them in the lower shelves of your refrigerator. Be attentive to the humidity levels of your refrigerator. Check if there is moisture and condensation around your plants as it can affect their quality.

But it is important that the surrounding area doesn't become too dry. There's nothing that you could do in order to alter your fridge to store microgreens, you should always protect them by covering them with the help of a paper towel. This allows air to pass through while maintaining enough moisture. The last thing to remember is that you must be aware of the different types. The quality of the seeds, as well as the conditions they were cultivated in and the method in which they were harvested can all impact the length of time your microgreens remain fresh, how long they'll stay and how abundant they are of nutrients.

If stored correctly the microgreens you have stored will last between two and three weeks. But, as this greatly is dependent on the particular plant, the best method to know the time you should keep each species in the refrigerator is to examine the crop it self.

How to incorporate microgreens into Your Daily Diet

In order to incorporate microgreens correctly into your daily diet it is important to consider selecting the appropriate method to consume them can affect the nutritional benefits you'll reap. The fact that they contain a lot of nutrients doesn't mean they will give you success unless you consume them correctly.

Although all research confirms that microgreens are basically nutrients that are a bomb and calling them superfoods is a good idea and gaining benefits from their antioxidant content is a matter of including them in your diet regularly and continuously.

This will increase your immunity, and lower the chance of suffering from diabetes, heart disease and obesity as well as hypertension. If you don't keep a regular schedule in your intake of microgreens, it's possible that you'll miss any specific results. It is vital to use them regularly given how simple and inexpensive it is to cultivate microgreens at home. Here are a few ways to include microgreens in your eating habits.

Salads

The first tip is to consume microgreens in fresh form in salads. Microgreens are the healthiest when eaten fresh. The less

103

processing you do to them in the process, the more nutrients remain. Their delicate flavors also remain potent if you consume the microgreens right after you harvest them. Cooking microgreens can deplete their nutrients so making up creative fresh recipes using raw vegetables is the best option. For instance, the sunflower plant, a small , lemony-green-looking plant, is a great ingredient to any salad.

Sandwiches and wraps

You can then make wraps and sandwiches using freshly picked herbs. They can be used to make intense, sweet spicy, and overall amazing flavors that will load your meals with nutrition. To achieve this, radish-colored greens are typically the most delicious condiments because they complement other fresh fruits and meats.

Fresh microgreens are great for adding an extra kick to wraps and sandwiches but you must make sure that these recipes are healthy and light with a focus on greens and vegetables instead of meats, breads and other toppings.

Meals cooked in the kitchen

Cooking using microgreens. There are numerous varieties of microgreens that can retain many nutrients when cooked. But, remember that the best advice is to add them to the dish towards the close of cooking and to not let them be exposed to temperatures that are high for more than a minute. Because these plants are safe to consume raw and cooking does nothing to increase the flavor You can also consider adding microgreens that are raw to dishes that are already cooked. They're great to mix with pasta, fried dishes as well as for side dishes.

Juices and Smoothies

Another way to consume microgreens is by using them to make smoothies and juices. If you're not a big lover of eating raw vegetables Juices and smoothies are a great method to incorporate them into your everyday food regimen. To this end the wheatgrass variety has proven to be one of the more sought-after. If you mix microgreens into the mix of your favourite leafy greens, veggies, as well as fruits, they'll give you the unique flavor you like. You can also make juices with microgreens on their own.

Be aware that you'll need 1 part of plants and 3 parts of water to make refreshing drinks that have sufficient nutrients.

Cooking Guide to the Best Nutrient Preservation

One of the most frequently asked questions constantly asked is whether microgreens can be considered safe to consume raw. In general, it's believed that microgreens that are raw are safe to consume on a daily basis. But, eliminating the germs prior to eating is crucial to reduce the chance of contracting parasites, fungi or bacteria as well as others harmful microbes.

Cooking microgreens is sure to remove them of valuable nutrients and enzymes. Water-soluble vitamins are also depleted. To ensure that your microgreens are as healthy to consume fresh as you can it is essential to ensure the cleanliness of the containers you grow in and wash them thoroughly prior to use. If you follow the rules to ensure the proper refrigeration, you'll lower the risk of mold and bacteria that may be growing within your plant. The plants can last up to a few weeks, while preserving their flavor and freshness (Mir et al. 2017).

The ideal way to eat microgreens is in their raw form. In this condition they have the highest amount of nutrients, and also have the strongest flavor. But, you can also make microgreens at home, so they aren't boiling them. If you don't wish to include fresh microgreens in your food, you can allow them to steam for a few minutes.

It is best to do this just a few minutes prior to when you remove the pot from the stove. In this way, your vegetables retain their freshness and taste while also preserving the essential nutrients.

In addition to microgreens in your meals, you are able to utilize leaves and stems provided you clean them off to remove any leftover debris and germs. The decision on whether or not to use the roots will depend on the kind of microgreen you're using. You can also mix your greens before adding them to your dishes, or crush them to release more aroma and flavor. Remember to mix as many varieties you'd like!

In this light In this regard, we'll present you with a few recipes that make use of microgreens. Next, you'll find the instructions to incorporate microgreens into your meals every day.

Tips and ideas for delicious meals

It is possible to enhance any meal with microgreens. They can add flavor that you like and adding spice to your most popular food items. In this article we'll offer you easy and easy ways to include microgreens into your everyday eating habits. The following are the easiest methods to transform any meal into a body-building treat:

Microgreen Pizza. It's an uncomplicated dish and we're not opposed to it in terms of healthy eating. However, topping a normal pizza with sausage, cheese and pepperoni does not make for the most digest-friendly food. Instead, substituting the fatty ingredients with microgreen arugula onions, basil or spinach could produce a delicious treat and healthy food.

It's not recommended to bake microgreens with the pizza or else you'll end up losing the majority of the nutrients. Instead, sprinkle the quantity you'd like in within a couple of minutes prior to taking the pizza from the oven. This will provide them with a delicious crunch, without degrading the nutritional value. You could make sure to season the pizza by adding fresh microgreens in case you'd like!

Burgers that contain microgreens. Burgers, unfortunately, have a bad reputation as being unhealthy. However, if you make them with microgreens such as arugula and kohlrabi as well as cabbage, they'll be bursting with rich flavors that quickly compensate for the absence of calories that come from carbs such as buns or cheese.

Delicious pesto. In addition to onions and basil it is possible to add pea shoots and sunflowers to make a delicious but healthy and nutritious pesto. This sauce can be used as a complement to pasta, or as a dressing for salads. It is also possible to use this pesto to spice up wraps and sandwiches.

Microgreen salsa. Salsa is a different dish designed for the imagination and the variety. What ever microgreen you pick from lemongrass to lemongrass cinnamon basil, sunflower or even more spicy ones like peppercress, you could simply include them in the dish to create your own recipe that is authentic to you. So, you'll end up coming up with a delicious recipe that's great with quesadillasand chips, tacos, tortillas, and other dishes.

Microgreen guacamole. By adding microgreen sunflowers to your normal guacamole will make a healthy dip to serve with chips or tacos. Of course, feel you are free to use any type of plant you want! It is also possible to include this guacamole in wraps, salads, sandwiches or any other dish you like.

Microgreen pancakes. If you're a fan of the pancakes you eat every day then you'll be able to find pea shoot microgreens to be an excellent option to add to your breakfast. Blend the plant by including chives, and other tasty greens to the batter. This will create an amazing pancake! Also, if making a meal for kids who tend to be averse to vegetables, as many do this is a great method to disguise them into an enjoyable dinner.

Microgreen pasta sauces. It's simple to transform the typical pasta sauce into something that is a treat to your blood vessels as well as your immune system, similar to the taste buds. Arugula, lemongrass, basil garlic, zucchini and many others provide delicious flavor to many sauces that range from Bolognese to pesto, and carbonara. There's no standard in the matter of including microgreens in pasta sauces. It's up to you to decide the quantity depending on your preference and preferences, and choose between crushing, mixing or even incorporating them in sauces. Additionally, putting the plant into sauces while they're cooking for less than one minute, will increase the flavor without compromising the nutritional value.

Microgreen Omelet. An omelet for breakfast with some microgreens is a fantastic option to fill your breakfast by providing precious proteins as well as vitamins and iron. If you add some delicious greens such as Microgreen spinach and onions and basil, to your simple egg, you'll receive an abundance of nutrients prior to your morning run or exercise. This will prepare you to have a productive day by increasing your energy levels and concentration at work. Additionally, the taste of this dish will add an exotic flavor and Mediterranean to a plain breakfast. Microgreens can be added to your omelet, by mixing them in the eggs before cooking or crushing them before adding them to the dish.

Microgreen soup. Soups are an excellent method to hydrate prior to having a delicious meal. Additionally, they're an excellent way to fight against viruses when you're sick, and improve your immune system. In order to include microgreens in your soap, make sure to add them after the food is cooked to preserve the highest amount of nutrients. Let the soup slow cool as the valuable plants heat inside the pot, exchanging flavor and nutrients. Sunflower onions, beans and lemongrass, basil carrots, radish, and other microgreens that you like can make an ideal option to add to your soup.

In this chapter, you've have learned more about the benefits of adding microgreens to your eating habits. Now that you know this information you are now able to enjoy the wonderful crops with the confidence that you'll be able to utilize them correctly and preserve their health benefits. It will make the effort worthwhileas you'll be able to observe the health benefits of regular usage.

Then, you were taught how to keep the microgreens you buy in your home, to keep them fresh flavor, texture, and nutritional value. The best method of refrigerating microgreens is to store the bags in plastic and protect them from temperature and moisture. It's recommended to keep your microgreens as far from the cooling source as you can, and to ensure that the temperature of your refrigerator at a minimum of 40 degrees Fahrenheit.

This chapter you've learned how to cook microgreens. Although there are some plants that can handle high temperatures but the majority don't have the right characteristics to cook and bake. Instead, you can include them in a dish that is already cooked and allow them to let their flavors release and steam when the food is cooling down. You also discovered that you can mix the greens with your sauces and juices to enhance the flavor of meals that are normally prepared.

Chapter 6: Start Your Own Hydroponic Garden

Numerous websites and sites on the Internet sell hydroponic systems for large amounts of dollars. However, it's less expensive to purchase the supplies you require and then build your own. While buying a kit comes with advantages, if you purchase and construct your own components, you can alter your design whenever and wherever you'd like.

The main benefit of purchasing the kit is the fact that it includes all the instructions. But, you could spend less money on a hydroponics system and make use of this guide, which contains pictures and instructions to guide you.

Are you curious about what you've learned about hydroponic gardening thus far? Are you ready to start your garden to hydroponics and apply the principles into action?

If you are developing your own hydroponic system, it's generally suggested to utilize an organic medium. This is a common practice that supports making use of an ebb and flow. Although a wick system can be very affordable and simple to set up, it is difficult to modify over time , and could result in poor results. There's a concern over whether the plants are getting the correct balance of nutrients If they are not, it may be challenging to modify the flow of nutrients.

This is why many hydroponic systems at home are low and even high. The majority of hydroponic gardens as well as the majority of traditional kindergartens, come with all the required equipment to set up a home-based system.

Growing hydroponically is in essence, that a farmer doesn't use soil for development. In the present it is the Latin word hydroponics refers to working water.

Always take your time researching the different aspects to increase chance of success. Every gardening activity can produce unfavorable results, and the process can dramatically increase your odds of success.

How will we use the method?

Our hydroponics system moves water from reservoir (container) via pipes or hoses until the point at which roots of plants are suspended. The roots soak up the water and nutrients since the flow of nutrients and water flows into the bottom of the container, where the plants are located. The nutrients and water return to the reservoir and the cycle is repeated. This is known as"the NFT method. NFT means nutritive film technology. It is the process of nutrients and water continuously moving across the roots. Water flows in pipes or channels, however we'll be using the rectangular container.

What medium to use?

Many hydroponic mediums are available and each is able to work with the other. I would recommend using clay rocks as my medium since they are able to help the plant grow and provide enough space to allow the roots of one another. I've seen other hydroponic systems made of Rockwool as an insulation. It is very effective because it's light. Therefore any lightweight and "airy" medium performs similarly.

How much attention is required?

If you begin with an undeveloped plant already developed root systems, more attention is required as you have to lead the root through the soil as well as through the pots in order to get water that has nutrients. If you purchase an existing plant with mature roots, you are able to gently push them through pots till they are able to reach the water and the nutrients.

Then, you might need to change the water in order to keep it in good condition. If you'd like you could also check that your system isn't running and conduct the "maintenance test."

Step 1. Materials

1. Two containers

It should be wide and deep (this helps to preserve the nutrients as well as water). Mine measured 58cm 39 cm and 19.5 cm (length length x width height/depth)One ideal is flat, and the dimension will depend on the amount of plants you want to plant (this keeps the plantsand the pots and the nutrients and water flow through the pots). The dimensions of mine were 38 cm by 28.5 cm in size and 17.5 centimeters (length length x width height/depth)

2. Mesh pots: It depends on the amount of posts you'd like to have and the amount of plants you'd like to cultivate

3. It is preferential to plant that have a root system established, not simply seeds (this method reduces the need for maintenance).

4. An air pump

* Model: AP-30

* Power 4 Watts

* Voltage: 220-240 volts

* Frequency: 50 Hertz

* Pressure: 0.015 MPa

* Capacity 3.5 milliliters/minute

5. A total of six meters

6. Stones for ventilation

7. A water pump

* Model: Aqua-Power 200

* Power 4 Watts

* The flow rate is 200 liters per hour.

* Maximum height: 0.60 meters

8. A method

9. Nutrients

Phase 2: Create Your Pot Holes

1. Find the lid for the container you'd like your jars to be able to sit on.

2. Put the lid of the dish on the lid's top upside down, and draw it using pencil (use the pictures above to make it clearer).

3. Set the pot on the top of the cover facing the other way and draw a circle with the pencil. Make sure this circle is within the circle that you traced upside down.

4. You can do this with as many pots you can manage.

5. You should finish with four circles. These result in two holes. Take the examples above for comparing yours with. They'd like to look like doughnuts.

6. In the smaller circle, you made an opening. Get a saw, start cutting that smaller circle.

7. After cutting small circles, begin cutting lines of lines that extend toward the larger circle. This will result in tiny "leaves," which better keep the pots in place.

8. Then, push through the holes in the bottom of the pans. My first attempt did not fit which is why I had to put the lid into the oven to cook the plastic. I pushed my pots through the holes, and waited until the plastic was cool.

Step 3: Set Your Air Pump

1. Take the 6-meter tube. Because the tube doesn't require stretching very far I

cut two pieces of tube that measure 80 cm.

2. Prior to connecting the pipe and the pump and connecting the air pump with an outlet and be sure that the air pump is pumping. If that isn't the case, then the fan that is responsible for aspirating the air could be blocked or there could be a failure of the pump. If it isn't working don't put any substance in the water for safety reasons.

3. Connect the two parts of hose together to connect them to your air compressor. The air pump you have may be from a different manufacturer or model, however I was able configure my own without assistance.

4. There are holes to be made within the tank in which there is water. You then have to run your hose into these holes.

5. Connect your stones for ventilation with the same air hose connected to the air pump.

6. Be sure that the air compressor is connected to an outlet before putting the stones for aeration in the water.

7. Then, place the aeration stones in the water, making sure they're completely covered with water.

8. Your venting stones should create bubbles.

Step 4: Setting Up Your Water Pump

1. Cleanse the pump with pure tap water prior to installing it into the system.

2. Make a hole in the container made of plastic where you'll want to hold the water. To accomplish this, I punched tiny holes using the screwdriver, and then I drilled.

3. I cut off a section of the hose that measured 6 meters and I pushed it into the hole. I then connected it to the water pump as well as the container to hold my pots.

4. The hoses were not able to pass through the holes or into the water tank, which is why I had to use an extremely strong glue to stop leaks.

5. To make sure it is working properly, make sure to fill the container up with water, then turn off the motor. The pump should move all the liquid through the hose the point where it is supposed to flow.

Step 5 Return the water to its Beginning

1. You can cut your 6-meter-long hoses into 6 distinct pieces. They should be long enough to allow them to flow between the "pot container" to their "water container."

2. Make six holes in you "pot container" and six holes into the lid on the lid of your "water container."

3. Place six tubes in each hole and then connect them to connect the "pot container" to the "water container." Because my tubes didn't precisely fit into these holes, I needed to attach them. I didn't put the holes inside the lid as there is no chance that water will get to this point.

4. To determine if it is working to determine if it works, put water in your "pot container" and let it move through the pipes to"the "water container."

Step 6: A Functioning Hydroponics System

After filling the tank with water, and then starting the pumps the hydroponic system has to be functional.

Step 7: Place Your plants in pots

1. Make sure you fill the top of the pots with medium, and allow enough room so that your root can flow over the nets and into the water.

2. Make sure to wash off any dirt that has accumulated on the roots using warm water. Be sure that the water is not hot or cold, because it could harm the plants and cause them to die.

3. Place your plants carefully inside the containers. Make sure the roots are able to pass through the soil and are in contact with the water flowing through the system.

4. Place the remainder of your media over and around the plant's base to provide it with the stability you require.

The amount of nutrients you can add to your hydroponic setup is dependent on the kind of plant you're cultivating. The majority of stores have a nutritional package that has the majority of the nutrients that they require.

Although nutrients aren't essential to the growth of your plants this is recommended since it can increase productivity of plants. Also, there is less chance that your plants will die by using nutrients.

Some herbs , like dill, chives and oregano don't require nutrients to survive. But, other herbs like basil need magnesium as a mineral.

Step 8 Step 8: Maintenance

* If you replace the water frequently, nutrients are also removed which is why you must change the nutrients.

* I recommend doing an examination several times per day to be sure that nothing has was done to your system or equipment for example, B. A leak.

When the plant's roots get excessively long and grow over the edge of the water I suggest replanting the plant since you do not need to keep it watered. If you put only the roots of a few (1-2 centimeters) into the water they should be good.

Chapter 7: What Is Their Real Nutritional Benefits

Micro-greens are popping up all over salads and sandwiches, and yet they're still delicious.

"Microgreens appear like tiny sprouts, and are a type that is a vegetable" states Monica Auslander Moreno, RD with RSP Nutrition. "There are around 60 varieties." Particularly, they are seeds that are harvested during the initial phase of growthwhich can originate from various plants like broccoli, cauliflower, cabbage and many more.

The most appealing part? Microgreens can be as much as 35 to forty times as active with phytochemicals as mature counterparts, as per research published by the Journal of Agricultural and Food Chemistry.

Micro-greens certainly live up to their title since they're so tiny that you can incorporate them into many dishes and not even recognize the micro-greens.

MicrogreensPolyphenols are compounds that have antioxidant properties.

They prevent free radicals from creating inside your body. They are molecules or atoms which can trigger chronic illness and cause cell damage.

Diets high in polyphenols have been linked to increase the risk of developing Alzheimer's disease, cancer as well as heart diseases.

Microgreens are nutrient-dense than mature varieties of the same plant or herb.

They collect all the vitamins and minerals that you'd find in a whole leaf of cabbage or lettuce and put them in a small container.

The majority of vegetables are rich in a myriad of vitamins and minerals that you can keep in mind: Vitamin A C, manganese, folate and many more.

They have the same kinds of nutrients as their micro-green counterparts.

Micro-greens can produce between 4 to 40 times more nutrients per gram than full-grown vegetables.

Just a handful of micro-greens every week will help in meeting your nutritional requirements.

Microgreens are easy and convenient.

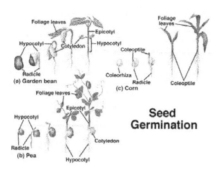

Seed Germination

Microgreens can be grown at home, even if you have not had a garden in the past. You can grow them even when you reside in an apartment, providing you with easy access to healthy food at any time you require it.

With a modest investment in a few plants, soil, or tray, you can enjoy healthy micro-greens for months to be.

They're ready for eating in only one or two weeks, and you can cultivate them all year long. It doesn't matter what the weather outside and you don't need to worry about mosquitoes or insects.

Growing your food will help reduce the carbon footprint too because you don't have to travel for thousands of miles just to reach your destination.

Microgreens are healthy salads that are sitting in your windowsill that you can eat and pick anytime. You can't get more fresh than this!

Microgreens can boost your Heart Well-being: Heart Disease is the most common cause of deaths within the US and is the cause of one of every six deaths.

However, by making changes to your diet, for instance, including more microgreens, you can reduce the chance of becoming a statistic.

Consuming more vegetables, in general, has been linked with an increased risk of suffering from heart attack and coronary disease. Microgreens aren't an one-off exception to that.

One of the most effective micro-greens for heart health are the red cabbage.

Microgreens and red cabbage have been proven to lower LDL cholesterol levels by 33 percent and triglycerides by 23 percent and weight gain of 17 percent, in the test on rats.

Microgreens aren't a magic treatment. If you mix these with other changes like an improved lifestyle that includes daily exercise and a balanced and balanced diet, you can dramatically improve your well-being. Particularly later in your life.

Microgreens can reduce the risk of chronic illness. Inflammation is a major risk factor for developing a disease within the body.

Microgreens and vegetables consumption has been proven to reduce inflammation markers and lower the chance of developing various forms of cancer.

They are also linked to an increased risk of developing type 2 obesity and diabetes.

Consuming a variety of micro-greens will ensure you are getting the nutrients you require.

Take care to consume micro-greens of various colors because different colors of fruit and vegetables are a reflection of phytochemicals that are beneficial compounds in addition to other micronutrients.

Red vegetables contain lycopenewhich is an antioxidant that is potent.

The yellow and orange vegetables are rich in carotenoids, such as beta carotene and lutein that the body converts into vitamin A.

Purple and blue vegetables are rich in anthocyanin, which can shield cells from injury.

Green vegetables have a range of phytochemicals, such as saponins, indoles and carotenoids.

White and brown vegetables, such as garlic have allicin that has antibacterial properties.

They lower the risk of developing heart disease.

The high blood pressure can be an important risk of heart disease and the good news is that plants-based foods like microgreens possess positive impacts for blood pressure. "Any plant-based fiber or vitamin K diet will help lower blood pressure" claims Auslander Moreno. This is in addition to other blood pressure treatments recommended by your physician Of course.

We could be helping fight cancer

Auslander Moreno says that plants such as micro-greens possess anti-cancer properties. In addition, research published in The Journal Future of Oncology found that sulforaphane, the chemical found in microgreen broccoli, may have the potential to treat stem cell cancer.

They can help improve the immune system.

If you feel like sniffles are starting to appear Do yourself a favor and prepare an enticing salad. "Any vegetables can help fight inflammation and can have a positive effect on the immune system," says Auslander Moreno. Microgreens pack lots of these essential nutrients into the form of a bag that is easy to eat.

They're helping improve eyesight

Increase your intake of leafy greens that includes micro-greens. According to the research of Auslander Moreno they contain luteinwhich is the phytochemical that is involved in vision security.

Research by Frontiers of Plant Science suggests that the content of lutein in microgreens could help the eyes to reduce the intensity of light -- something that many office workers believe could cause headaches or migraines.They're increasing the risk of constipation.

Micro-greens can accelerate the process of using the bathroom, as part of the overall diet that is healthy. "Any fiber is a great way to reduce symptoms of constipation" Says Auslander Moreno.

They're helping fight digestive diseases.

As per Auslander Moreno substantial prebiotic fiber content found in micro-greens can help feed friendly probiotic organisms within your digestive tract. In the journal Gut Microbes backs that up these prebiotic fibers help in the growth of intestinal bacteria that are associated with healthy health and well-being.They could be helping reduce cholesterol levels.

Chapter 8: Microgreens Cultivation

MIcrogreens as a term is the result of the process that result from the germination of seeds and the growth of their roots in water. They are harvested prior the developing into leaves. They are designed to be consumed in full and include the seed. The term "micro-greens" does not have a specific legal definition, but it is used to refer to the young , tender seedlings that can be eaten that are derived from seeds of different kinds of crops, vegetables, herbs as well as aromatic herbs and plants that grow spontaneously.

The seeding density

Large seeds = 1 seed/cm2.

(e.g. chickpeas, peas, corn, etc.)

Small to medium seeds = 2 seeds/cm2.

(e.g. radish, wheat, etc.)

Very tiny seeds = 4 seeds/cm2.

(e.g. Arugula, turnip top chicory, broccoli, etc.).

From an agronomic as well as commercial standpoint, the selection of species that can be grown to produce of micro-agents is closely dependent on the availability of high-quality seeds, which are distinguished by their the homogeneous and high-quality germinability, not treated with chemicals, and hygiene-safe, but also accessible at a low cost. Additionally, what's crucial is choosing plants that can be grown all year long and are able to meet specific environmental and thermal needs, particularly in the stage of germination. Another important commercial aspect is the post-harvest or shelf duration for the item.

There are a variety of plants that are microgreen. The differences are evident from the beginning of the cultivation. They are derived from specific seeds and above-ground cultivation methods (e.g. with coconut fiber) in protected areas, like greenhouses, where you can control the variables that affect their development (light, temperature, and humidity). So the treatments to protect against pests are slowed down or even not used at all and no fertilizers are employed. The microgreens grown using a traditional method are were harvested ahead of time when they start to grow their first leaves, which is just 10 to 20 days after the sowing. Microgreens are advantageous in that they are also sold in their entirety, along with the growing substrate in general: It is the one who eats the microgreens that cut them, only a few minutes prior to use. This is essential since it ensures a longer time for the microgreens to last and guarantees a superior quality in terms the freshness and nutritional value. Freshly harvested microgreens are then cleaned, placed into small plastic containers, and immediately refrigerated , and kept at a low temperature until they are consumed. Because they are live seedlings they are stored within the fridge for 10 to 15 days. Sowing is usually done manually spreading the seeds over the top of the substrate. The process of germination should take place in darkness and at temperatures that are suitable that the plant species requires (15-20 degree Celsius). In order to produce micro-organisms, seeds do not require be placed at the depth and also to ensure that when it germinates, the sprout is affected with the substrate. But, during this time the seeds must be kept cool to ensure that it is able to germinate completely Therefore during the period of two or three days following sowing, the trays for cultivation can be covered without touching the seeds with such as the black plastic film in order to increase temperatures and, consequently, the speed of germination and ensuring good humidity within the germinating area. After germination has occurred the cover should be removed. Contrary to common leafy vegetables, they are that are grown in the fields, and that, after being mature can be eaten.

The seeds that can be cultivated at any time of the year, sprout without the use of any fertilizers or parasites because of their short time to grow This is in keeping with the intention of providing the authenticity of the product through its early harvest. In this portion of the book, we're going to discuss all aspects of cultivating at home to assist you in the process of making your own, not only microgreens. To accomplish this it is important to be aware about synergistic farming, and to properly mix different varieties of vegetables that are compatible with them. you'll learn how to plant your own garden in your home whether you grow microgreens or not.

The Synergistic Agriculture

It has been demonstrated that certain plants aid each other to grow but others hinder one the other by weakening. Synergistic agriculture is founded on these fundamentals. It is a natural and eco-friendly method of cultivating, and is recommended to use when you are planning to set the vegetable garden or a garden in your backyard.

Synergistic gardening is a cultivating method that is based on the concept of reciprocity. When the soil helps it grow they make fertile soil using organic chemical residues, in conjunction with microorganisms, bacteria earthworms and fungi.

The results of this technique have a distinct quality, a distinct taste with a different energy level and greater resistance to the disease-carrying agents because of this method of cultivating the energy returns towards the soil. This improves the soil's processes of self-fertility. This makes agriculture a viable human activity.

Natural agriculture is founded on observation of the natural world and accepting responsibility for its actions. Simple solutions are picked and interventions are restricted to only the most essential practicesthat do not interfere with the natural cycle. Natural agriculture is also an eco-friendly method, which aims at not just cultivating plants, but also the consideration for our environment. "We don't inherit the world from our forefathers We have it borrowed from the children of our generation. It is our responsibility to repay it to them" As stated in the proverb of those of American Indians.

Synergistic gardening, which is a method that is organic, was a technique of cultivation created by Spanish farmers and permaculturists Emilia Hazelip.

This is built on idea that is widely supported by most recent microbiological research that, while soil is what makes plants grow, they also create fertile soil by the organic residues that they leave and the chemical activity they perform along with microorganisms, earthworms, fungi, and bacteria.

The fruits and vegetables that result from this method have a distinct flavor, different quality as well as a different level of energy and higher resistance to diseases-carrying agents. because of this method of cultivating it is possible to return more energy back to soils than utilized, encouraging the process of self-fertility of the soil and making farming an environmentally sustainable human endeavor.

Emilia Hazelip was a Spanish Agronomist from Spain. She was a pioneer in sustainable and long-lasting agricultural practices, developing and designing methods of cultivating synergistic farming, the outcome of the adaptation to Mediterranean environment of the natural agricultural climate developed by the Japanese microbiologist Masanobu Fukuoka, and Permaculture developed created by Bill Mollison and David Holmgren.

Emilia Hazelip trained in organic agriculture at the time in California in the early sixties . Then from 1978 onwards she has shown interest in the natural farming practices of Masanobu Fukuoka after her reading of the book The Straw Thread

Revolution. If we alter the way we cultivate the food we eat, then alter our diet, and we transform society, and we alter our attitudes.

Straw Thread Revolution Straw Thread Revolution explains how to be aware of the connections between everything that affect us, their causes and how to take responsibility for the things you are aware of. When Fukuoka speaks of the farming practices that he calls "not taking," a Westerner might be able to easily remember Matthew 6:26 "Follow through your vision the beings who fly across the sky They do not sow or reap, or have barns for putting on top of each other. It is God The Heavenly Father who is the one who feeds them.

There is actually an intimate connection between the divine and nature and divine providence, a connection that technological technology is able to destroy by imprisoning nature and rendering providence unusable. This book marks an important turning point in an era of liberation.

"The phrase Permaculture is a combination of "permanent agriculture" and "permanent culture" which means that no culture can last for very long without a sustainable base for agriculture and a land use ethics. The term is now well-known across the globe due to the book by Bill Mollison of the same title. It has been translated into all major languages The book has sold more than 80k copies across the globe. In the most extreme synergistic way, synergistic agriculture is the process of combining the knowledge of different fields (natural agricultural, climateology bio-architecture, ecology, botany) to create, harmoniously with nature an alternative path for happiness and wellbeing. The objective is to build an environmentally sustainable and economically viable system capable of meeting the demands and avoid any kind of pollution or exploitation and, consequently, long-term sustainable.

Four Principles of Synergy Agriculture Four Principles of Synergy Agriculture

1.No Tillage.

Complete absence of ploughing or other soil disturbance since the soil is created entirely by the the roots of plants, as well as the microfauna and fauna living beneath the soil.

It is the active part of soil where the most biochemical and biological activity is concentrated can be found at 30 centimeters. This is where oxygen is present, which is the active layer in the soil , where the best degradation of organic matter and the transformation into humus, upon which the farmer is able to intervene to achieve this, occurs. In soils where clay and silt dominate and clay is predominant, it is best to work for a minimum of 15 centimeters. In soils that are wet and have low temperatures the mineralization in organic matter can be slow, and it is evident that the loss in ammonia as well as carbon dioxide are minimal. This is the reason why the minimal work and hard sowing have been introduced to areas where the climate is humid and cool'.

The soil isn't tilled or disturbed, except at the beginning, in the construction of Pallets (flowerbeds). This helps to preserve its stratification (tissue structure) in order to preserve the actions of all kinds of living things present and ensure the continuity of the soil. The soil is viewed as an actual laboratory for biochemical research, where CO_2 storage is taking place. Not plowing the soil will prevent the soil from dispersing in the air after every plowing, adding to the greenhouse effect.

2.No contribution of fertilizers.

Fertilization of soil is constant because of the roots of plants that are never removed from the soil, and the use of mulching i.e. continuous organic cover. This is the reason for the development of the concept of the synergistic cultivation of only mulch, at the expense of any fertilizer. In reality the soil over the roots or around crops is covered by organic materials, like straw, that helps to insulate the soil, shielding it from heat and rain and also preventing the growth of weeds that threaten plants.

3.No synthetic treatment.

Fertility is provided through the organic layer of the soil. As it happens in nature in which the fallen leaves overly a layer which decomposes and forms the humus. This process can be replicated by our gardeners. We can reuse materials like straw leaves, bark, twigs and so on. Then, we place them over the ground. This ensures a steady humidity and temperature for plants and soil It also holds the water and other substances within the soil, which protects against the heavy rain and drying out. It also regulates and manages the growth of invasive wild plants.

Synthetic chemicals cannot be accepted because they are not renewable and natural. Pesticides are chemicals used to safeguard plants against insects (weeds) as well as fungi that fight off insects and diseases. Unfortunately, these chemicals do don't just protect us from undesirable species but they can also harm our health as well as the environment.

4.No Soil Compaction

To maintain soil fertility, it's important to build tunnels for an air-reflux. By leaving the plant's roots after the process, and not disrupting the activity of microorganisms and small animals allows you to build tunnels that are porous that soften the soil and prevents the death of underground life and the formation of an anaerobic atmosphere at the surface.

The soil will expand when we do not compact it. Compaction is the compressing of soil into smaller quantities due to the diminution of the space between them. It is typically followed by major modifications to the structural properties and behavior of soil, in addition to its water and thermal balance, and properties of its gaseous and liquid phase.

Flowers, vegetables aromatic, medicinal, or fruit trees can be placed in close succession, making the environment as diverse and productive as is possible, that is suitable for animals to live in and beneficial insects.

The associations studied can enable us to limit parasite attacks and to build an active system in which plants are actively involved in the mutual health and are a part of the soil's natural fertility.

It is recommended to cultivate at three or more botanical families, primarily by ensuring the continuous presence of the liliaceae (excellent repellents against insects as well as fungal disease) along with legumes (nitrogen-fixative). The selection of the plants is based upon the concepts of arrangement and association within space. Growing biodiversity as much as is possible helps in the growth of an ecosystem which regulates itself by utilizing a variety of synergies among living things.

The creation of a home Garden

Agriculture is the process of cultivating soil to produce products for animal and human food and the raw materials required for a variety of industries (cotton flax, flax, oilseeds and more.). It also covers the farming of livestock and forest management. There are three major areas that research is conducted in the field of agriculture that are related to the physical and environmental conditions that impact animal and plant production. It also includes, among other disciplines, agronomy animal husbandry, and forestry. The second is the aim of the people who work in agriculture, and is the subject of rural sociology. The third concern the actions of State agencies and operators in relation to these goals and conditions, and is specifically related to the economy and agriculture policy.

Home Garden is a concept that has been attracting increasing numbers of people. If you want to become an urban farmer and have tried your hand in growing aromatic herbs and small vegetable plants in your terrace or garden There is a fresh method of growing your seeds without pesticides or in extremely-small space.

The garden for vegetables will be fully covered in mulch and soil that must be ventilated and full of humus. The plants are continually recycled, leaves are removed, and the manure plants that are green are buried to supply nutrients to the harvest in summer; some fennel, carrot and dill plants are allowed to flower to attract wasps that feed on parasites , and some tomatoes and cucumbers that grow out of the compound pile is transferred across the fence.

It is not a plan to organize the garden in strict rows. Instead, it appears as an interspersed arrangement of bushes, flowers, creepers, flower beds as well as herbs, tiny trees (lemon Mandarin) as well as a tiny pond. The paths are sinuous , and the flower beds can be circular, keyhole-shaped and raised, or spiral, or sunken.

It doesn't matter what technique you choose to design your garden, whether that's double spading the flower beds or just mulching them with straw and newspaper. The main thing is to choose a method that will satisfy you. For lazy people Full mulching is the best option. Perhaps someone else is suited for double mulching since they're young. This technique isn't something that is fixed but rather something that is adapted to the situation, the time of year, the inclination and conviction.

The most important thing is that you plan your garden in accordance with your frequency of visit as well as the size of the harvest and also to provide an array of plant species to help control insects. Even when we are planning a small space, such as the vegetable garden, we can apply the permaculture principles of placing the flower beds according to the amount of days they will be planted.

The steps to create of a bedstead based on the synergistic farming method comprise the design. This is the time that we look at the space available and gather data about exposure to the sun, temperature, winds and orientation, etc. And then, choose the design of the beds that will be enclosed.

The flowerbeds' preparation involves preparing the ground by constructing piles between 20 and 50 centimeters tall and 120 centimeters wide , on average, and 5 to 7 meters in length. Between one flowerbed and the next, there are walkways that are at minimum 50 centimeters in width. The next stage is the setting up of the raised flowerbeds where the plants will be grown. The design of the flowerbeds could be straight, curved , or mandala-shaped. Their function is to define the passages for humans and to keep from compacting the landscape. The suggested width for flowerbeds is 120cm, and there is no limit in the width. It is suggested to build passageways every 4-5 meters and with an average width of around 80 centimeters. The height however could be as high as an maximum of 30-40cm as higher elevations decrease the surface that can be used for cultivation. The pallets are constructed using the same soil that is used in the area where vegetables are created and drip irrigation systems is required to be set up on the pallets.

After you have designed the synergistic garden, and constructed the flower beds the drip irrigation system that will ensure that the plants receive water even during periods of extreme drought should be put in place to complete the installation.

It isn't difficult to create a garden system using drip fins that can reach every flower bed. If the synergistic garden is an approach to cultivating the land that is in harmony with its resources, naturally the way of utilizing of water has to be mindful and mindful. The most suitable method of irrigation for synergistic gardens is using a drip irrigation method that ensures the best utilization of water. It is absorbed slowly and thoroughly into the soil. This saves amounts of water required. Furthermore, this system can prevent wetting the leaves, thus reducing the possibility of plants getting the fungi.

Chapter 9: Marketing Strategies

How to Request Certification

Another way to increase demand is to grow the micro-greens you have organically. Organic foods are extremely fashionable in our society today and especially with those who are conscious of their health.

The health-conscious consumers who purchase organic food are likely to be those who are concerned enough about health and wellness to research about microgreens, for instance, and then decide to buy and consume these microgreens. One way to prove to them that you're growing organically is to become something known as "certified organic".

The first step you have to do in order to get certified organic is to research for a certifier that is USDA-accredited. This is crucial because if you choose a person to examine your growth techniques but they aren't USDA-accredited, you won't be certified organic based on the results of their inspection even if have done everything in correctly.

If you locate an agent that is certified they will be sent an application along with the fee to complete the application by mail. The price of these fees varies based on two elements: the certifying agency you select and how big your farm is. Certain certifying companies charge more for applications than other. In the same way, farms of different sizes are more expensive than other farms too. Cost of an organic certification can range from 200 to 1500 dollars, which includes application fees, inspection fee, and annual license fees.

Generally speaking, the bigger the farm in size, the more it will cost. In this regard, it might be beneficial to get certified organic while your farm is small. It is possible to expand in the future but this can enable you to become certified for a bit lower cost at the moment.

When the certifying agent has received the application form and payment They will review the application. They will scrutinize every detail you submit to confirm that you are actually cultivating your microgreens to meet the standards they require.

Naturally, you'll need to be sure you're actually adhering to the guidelines. In order to begin this process you must at a minimum know the requirements. Agriculture marketing from the USDA department has a wonderful interactive video that will show you how to make your organic farm if you'd prefer a visual way to begin studying. We will also provide this information on our website.

Once you have confirmed that your microgreen farm is produced organically and the certifying agency approves your application, they'll make an appearance at your site. They will visit your location to examine and ensure all the information you provided on your application is true. If you are actually adhering to the rules in order to be natural the visit shouldn't cause any issues in any way. But, if the agent arrives and observes that you are spraying weeds with Roundup in a jug, your visit is likely to not take the course you would like it to.

The agent will then return to their office and take a look at the specifics of your visit along with the application. They will then determine if your farm is in compliance with the USDA guidelines to allow the farm to qualify "certified organic". This is the ultimate decision on your application.

When the final decision has been taken, the certifying agent will get in touch with you to provide an answer. If you didn't get through, your agent will explain the reason for this and your application will be rejected.

If you are able to meet the requirements of the certifying agency they will issue an official certificate that confirms that your product is certified organic. It is then possible to apply this label to your marketing campaigns to demonstrate to the public that your product is organic. It's a label consumers can trust, which will increase the popularity of your products.

Marketing Tips

Once you've got the certifications to market your microgreens to make a profit How do you locate people who will buy your microgreens? Here are some strategies to market your microgreens to a variety of potential customers.

Schools

In the beginning, we're going to begin looking at the different ways microgreens can be sold in certain areas. One location where you might consider selling your microgreens is an academic campus or in a university kitchen. Student meals that are healthy and nutritious are becoming more essential and receive lots of interest. Prepare to lower the cost of your food because you're selling in large quantities.

Hospitals

Another possibility for an ideal place to sell your microgreens is to private-owned hospitals. These hospitals are willing to go the extra mile to satisfy their customers. They may decide to include some fresh microgreens with their meals. Always make sure to talk to the chef, not the hospital's head. Send some samples or contact the person who is in charge of the meal plan.

Restaurants

Selling to various restaurants can be your most significant source of revenue. They generate steady sales. It is possible to grow microgreens in accordance with the instructions you receive with the cook. Contacting local chefs is essential to your business strategy. Offer the chef free samples , and return the following week to inquire about whether they enjoyed the experience and if they'd like to make an order. If not, give them other microgreens. The key is persistence. You should only offer them the highest microgreens of the highest quality.

Give them two choices of delivery: cutting or live microgreens. Send them a form with your contact information as well as any possible microgreens that you could cultivate. It is also possible to cold-call establishments.

Retail stores

Retail could be a great alternative where you can sell microgreens well. It is possible to contact health food stores to inquire whether they would like to place your product on their shelves. To accomplish this, you'll have to donate a portion of the proceeds for the shop.

But, it could be very beneficial to you as it allows that your item to sell for very little effort from your side. This will also enable the product you sell to be noticed by more people, which will make it more popular with the customers you can reach. To collaborate with an establishment that sells health foods, you can contact them and inquire whether they are interested in partnerships, or you can visit the store and give the store owner a few samples of your microgreens along with an inventory of your product.

The second choice is more personal and could be the better option. If you're welcoming and have a good product, the store might be more inclined to permit the sale of the product they carry at their store.

Farmers Markets

Markets for farmers is also an excellent opportunity. Not just for selling your microgreens but also to meet other sellers , and perhaps swap some of your microgreens in exchange for other products.

Being part of a group of others who are doing the same can result in greater knowledge and connections to sales opportunities for your business in the future.

As an example the stand that is near you offers mushrooms for sale to restaurant owners. He could introduce you to the restaurant's chef , and inform them that you're selling high-quality microgreens. This may result in more business opportunities.

There is a juice-making trend. Wheatgrass is one of the most popular microgreens that people juice. You just need an ice-cold press juicer and place wheatgrass in the hopper. Then, turn by hand or with electricity to make a nutritious juice. I'm sure a lot of people will stop by to take the juice!

Online

As you may have noticed the majority of items today are bought on online Internet rather than in-person. This is why you may want to sell your products on the internet.

An ideal method to achieve this is to establish a monthly or weekly subscription service to ensure that you're growing the same amount of microgreens every month , or every week. In this way, you'll be able to sell the microgreens regardless of. If you get people signing for your product, you'll be able to know exactly how many microgreens are required to be growing.

Social Media Marketing

People enjoy spending time on websites like Facebook as well as Instagram. They are using these websites to stay in touch with their acquaintances, but also are able to find new products advertised.

If you post images of your growing business or explain why you're doing what you're doing It can help customers to feel a personal connection to your company. If people feel a greater personal connection with your company and your brand, they are more likely to purchase from you instead of another company they do not know.

Even if you don't have any contact with them in person Social media can make them feel as if they are familiar with your brand , which could let them buy more products from your company than they might otherwise.

The most significant benefit of marketing via social media is the ability to run ads to those who are keen on healthy living and are in the region you're located in. This is an extremely effective marketing opportunity since the majority of microgreen growers do not spend time on marketing via social media. You can offer recurring subscription boxes on the social media platforms.

Create your own website

Building a website on your own is a breeze nowadays. It's easy to make one using WordPress and Shopify. The site could be filled with useful information to help your customers and clients find the information they're seeking. Customers can make purchases from this site or it could be a website that enlightens the public about your business.

Your website will show up in Google search results when someone searches for microgreens to purchase. This can assist you in acquiring new customers, too. A well-designed website can cost around 12 dollars for the domain name per year and 60 dollars hosting for the year. Find some instructional videos online about how to create your own website using WordPress It's easy!

Another aspect you have to be aware of regarding selling and marketing is how to manage your company.

If you're not able to monitor the business's sales it is difficult to know how your company is performing. It is difficult to know the types of profits you're earning in the absence of knowing the amount you're earning.

The ability to track your sales is extremely useful in determining the microgreens or clients that generated the highest amount of profits.

It will help you know the busy season and the low season. It will also allow you to identify which places generate the highest revenues. This will help you take planned trips or invest more effort into the most lucrative ways to earn money.

The first step is to have a method to record the products you're selling. A great tool is a spreadsheet. If you are using the spreadsheet, it is possible to store all of your sales into one spot.

Use Google Sheets to ensure you don't lose the data your computer decides you've been through enough.

If you input your data into Excel and then use Excel, you can determine your sales total and uncover patterns. It is possible to use this data to draw graphs, in order to visualise the information.

It's always an excellent idea to keep your receipts. If you keep your receipts, you'll always know the amount you have spent for your company. You can then type the numbers into a spreadsheet such as Excel. If you don't save receipts, it is possible to not remember certain charges. It's not a huge deal, however it's worth mentioning it.

If you fail to remember one expense, your figures are likely to be wrong, which the IRS isn't happy about. If you're not able to keep track of how much you've spent this could lead to some pretty serious penalties.

Making receipts can be quite simple and is something you must always keep in mind to ensure your business is running smoothly. Think about using a specific location to keep your receipts, and then place them in when you get them.

Set up a separate account for your bank for your business to ensure that your personal bank account isn't connected to the company bank account. This eliminates a number of headaches that are unnecessary during tax time.

Your venture may make some money, but remember you're time valuable. You could consider starting it as a side-job and, if it works out it's possible to go full-time.

Conclusion

We've reached the final page of this book , and there's nothing left to add. We've given you a range of resources and tips to help you get off your feet and grow your microgreens now, and we hope we have encouraged you in some way in the process! As we've said several times before microgreens are just getting started and if you're following this article, you've probably already realized the potential that this place in the market has.

However it's not all about money or making money. life should be about earning cash or managing a business microgreens are an excellent option to keep your day doing simple, fun activities that aid you in improving your health each day by doing something that can aid in improving your health and provide something special to the meals you eat regularly.

We urge you to continue and keep learning (along along with the plants) and get the most of the tools that you have at your disposal. Concentrate on what you do and putting your best effort into it and amazing opportunities to begin to manifest.

There's not much more we can impart to you however, before we say goodbye, we'd like to leave you with one last piece of advice . We hope you try your best to adhere to the advice.

You cannot master something by reading about it. you must try and test numerous times as often as you'd like before you begin to see the results you're looking for. It's perfectly normal and you must be sure to remember this. This isn't just a matter of microgreens. It also applies to all sorts of aspects of life.

Don't be disappointed in not being able to achieve infinite success on the very first go. It will happen however it's entirely your decision. Relax and ensure that you're having fun with the process. If you are disciplined and are optimistic eventually, things will begin to become more natural.

Happy Growing!